Praise for *JURAN: A Lifetime of Influence*

"Joe Juran has led the quality cause from its earliest days. His progressive influence via this enlightening text will be virtually endless."

> Robert W. Galvin
> Chairman of the Executive Committee
> Motorola

"As much as anyone in the field, Dr. Joseph M. Juran is a major influence in the business world's pursuit of quality. *Juran: A Lifetime of Influence* finally gives the great man his due. Quality gurus and greenhorns alike will find much to savor in this entertaining and educational book."

> Robert A. Lutz
> Vice Chairman
> Chrysler Corporation

"John Butman has captured the extraordinary spirit of one of America's most remarkable pioneers, Joseph M. Juran, in a wonderful text that reads almost like a novel. Here we get a true glimpse of some of the forces that have driven Dr. Juran for over 92 years and of his many breakthrough contributions to the world of business."

> A. Blanton Godfrey
> Chairman
> Juran Institute

"John Butman has beautifully crafted an insightful and highly readable biography of quality pioneer, Joseph M. Juran. The book provides an intimate look at Juran's personal life, while giving the reader a lucid understanding of his philosophy, teachings, and accomplishments. Both informative and inspirational, it's must reading for any devoté of quality."

> G. Howland Blackiston
> Executive Producer of the PBS television
> documentary, *An Immigrant's Gift*

"The author clearly describes the unique contributions that Dr. Juran made to the quality movement. The two most important keys to the success of any quality program are the emphasis on culture and human relations, and the knowledge of how-to's. Dr. Juran excelled in both."

Thomas H. Lee
President and Professor Emeritus
Center for Quality of Management
Massachusetts Institute of Technology

"The story of Joe Juran personalizes the history of quality in the twentieth century. He was part of the movement almost from the beginning—and remains so."

Robert W. Hall
Editor-in-Chief, *Target*
Association for Manufacturing Excellence

"John Butman has done a tremendous service by writing this well-documented, easy-to-read biography of a remarkable man in a critical period of the twentieth century. Many hitherto untold anecdotes give us insight into Dr. Juran's influence on society. I recommend it not only to quality professionals and business managers, but also to the general public as well."

Yoshinao Nakada
Technical Manager
Bell Laboratories
Lucent Technologies

"This biography affords us a rare look into the private life of a man who in a very real sense was the architect of Quality Management. The book was fascinating to me because it discerned the influences that combined to create Joe's rock hard idealism—an idealism that was always searching for the great truths and that had the chutzpah to declare to the world: 'Perfection is possible'!"

E. LaVerne Johnson
President and CEO
International Institute for Learning, Inc.

JURAN

JURAN
A LIFETIME OF INFLUENCE

JOHN BUTMAN

JOHN WILEY & SONS, INC.

New York • Chichester • Weinheim • Brisbane • Singapore • Toronto

This text is printed on acid-free paper.

Copyright © 1997 by John Butman.
Published by John Wiley & Sons, Inc.

Library of Congress Cataloging-in-Publication Data:

Butman, John.
  Juran : a lifetime of influence / John Butman.
    p. cm.
  Includes bibliographical references and index.
  ISBN 0-471-17210-3 (cloth : alk. paper)
    1. Juran, J. M. (Joseph M.), 1904– . 2. Industrial engineers–
United States–Biography. 3. Quality control–History. 4. Total
quality management. I. Title.
  TS140.J87B88 1997
  658.5'0092–dc21
    [B]   97–14194

Printed in the United States of America

10 9 8 7 6 5 4 3 2 1

Contents

The Japanese liked Deming because he had a list.

Peter Drucker

Deming had a philosophy, not a list.

Lloyd Dobyns

Dr. Juran's visit marked a transition in Japan's quality control activities from dealing primarily with technology based in factories to an overall concern for the entire management.

Jungi Noguchi

Deming was the philosopher. Juran was the trainer. I was the implementer.

A.V. Feigenbaum

Had Deming and I stayed home, the Japanese would have achieved world quality leadership all the same.

J. M. Juran

I am number one in Japan.

Peter Drucker

Preface:
The Pantheon

Q uality is an idea; it changes with time.
   As the world entered the twentieth century, quality implied an essential goodness of nature (a thing of great quality) or a special, usually expensive, grade of manufacture (high-quality goods).

In the second half of the century, quality escaped its burden of luxury and was liberated from its association with high cost. It emerged as a classless idea that comprises precision (expert execution of manufacture or service delivery), reliability (no failures or mistakes), usefulness (meets a need), and a positive response from those who encounter it (satisfaction and even enjoyment).

As the twenty-first century nears, the idea of quality has taken on an even richer, broader meaning. It is no longer considered to be a methodology for improvement and cost reduction primarily of industrial products and commercial services. We seek to apply quality methods to improve entire systems: organizations, governments, educational systems, the environment, national cultures.

This powerful idea has been shaped and refined, starting early in the twentieth century, through the efforts of a small number of quality advocates and practitioners. Their ideas catalyzed into dramatic action our natural inclination to improve; their methods and tools have enabled us to improve more quickly than we might have otherwise.

This book is the story of one of those quality proponents, Joseph Moses Juran. If there were a quality pantheon, Juran would be a charter member. William Edwards Deming and Walter A. Shewhart would stand beside him. Others, whose contributions are not deeply considered here (including Armand V. Feigenbaum, Kaoru Ishikawa, and Philip Crosby) would have their advocates.

Juran is distinguished by the breadth and depth of his knowledge, the clarity of his ideas, the practicality of his methods, the scope of his activity, and his extraordinary longevity as a major contributor to the field.

Juran provided the most precise and applicable definition of the elusive phenomenon we call quality. He defined two universal sequences of action steps, one for achieving *breakthrough,* one for achieving *control.* He articulated the Pareto Principle, which holds that a small percentage of factors in any situation will yield a large percentage of the effect. And Juran argued—forcefully and tirelessly—that a supportive organizational structure and management commitment are essential to the achievement of quality.

Juran's ideas, methods, and teachings have earned him a respect that borders on reverence from the quality community and have had a major impact on how we manage our businesses, how we create our products and services, and, indeed, upon the quality of our lives. "I think I am sitting with God," remarked one seminar attendee when he found himself seated at Juran's luncheon table.

Juran's life story and the story of quality are intertwined. His personal history has not been told before in print; a television documentary *An Immigrant's Gift* provides the only introduction to his life. The quality story has been told in pieces, through examinations of specific periods of activity (the 1920s, World War II, the 1980s), specific industries (most notably, the auto industry in such books as *The Reckoning* and *The Machine That Changed the World*) or in summary (such as Juran's own *A History of Managing for Quality*).

This book explores—through the story of Joseph Juran—the evolution of the quality movement in the twentieth century, primarily in the United States. It is, therefore, as much a biography of quality as it is of one person who helped define it.

JOHN BUTMAN

Boston, Massachusetts
April 1997

Joseph M. Juran, age 18, from the University of Minnesota publication "Gopher."

1

A World without Quality

(1904–1920)

What is so fascinating as the journey of a human creature through life?

Joseph Juran

OLD WORLD BOYHOOD

In the past three generations, each of the men of the Juran family seems to have taken one spectacular risk in his life.

Naftuli Juran, Joseph Juran's grandfather, emerged from the Carpathian Mountains one day, probably in the late 1860s, and settled in a tiny village nestled between the foothills and the Moldava River, in what is now Romania. Where Naftuli came from, who he was, why he was on the run—even his real name—no one now knows. He may have been a bank robber, a horse thief, a traveling teacher, or a young man fleeing from Russian Cossacks to escape conscription. Whatever the catalyst, Naftuli had taken a bold once-in-a-lifetime chance in crossing the pinnacled mountains and sudden gorges of the landscape we associate with Count Dracula, where wolves howl and few people live, to settle in a new region and pursue a new life. Naftuli came with a friend, Mordecai, and the two newcomers took temporary refuge with a local family named Juran, whose name they permanently borrowed.

The region was then part of the Austro-Hungarian empire (now Romania; see Figure 1.1) and under Austrian rule. The village, called Gurahumora (now Gura Humorului), had a small, but significant, Jewish population, which Naftuli joined. He married and started a family which grew to eleven children: eight girls and three boys. Joseph Juran's father, Jakob, was born in 1874.

Naftuli died young, leaving Jakob to be raised by sisters and aunts. He showed some promise at school and the family hoped he would become a scholar or a rabbi. But he much preferred cards to schoolwork, and he sought the company of Gentiles rather than Jews. After four years, he abandoned his studies and apprenticed to a shoemaker. Around 1900, Jakob left Gurahumora to set up shop in the more prosperous city of Braila, a shipping town on the Danube in southeastern Romania, where Jakob's sister and brother owned a restaurant. There,

Figure 1.1 Juran was born in what is now Romania.

Jakob fell in love with Gitel Goldenburg, a pretty, dark-haired girl who worked—as most dowry-less girls did—as a domestic, a house keeper. They married and their first son, Rudy, was born in 1901. Rebecca followed in 1903. Joseph Juran was born on December 24, 1904. (Juran selected his own middle name, Moses, when he was a teenager.)

Business did not flourish for Jakob in Braila so, in 1906, he moved his family back to Gurahumora and into a rough house next door to another sister and her prosperous husband, a metals merchant. It was a primitive house in the primitive village, with dirt floors, mud streets, and planks for sidewalks. As Juran grimly jokes, "They had no quality problems" in Gurahumora—there was no electricity, they had no automobiles. Here, Gitel gave birth to a fourth child, Nathan, in 1907.

Jakob took a dim view of Romania, where "nobles will always be noblemen, and shoemakers' sons will always be tradesmen," as he told his sons. Besides, the spread of factory-made shoes was beginning to cut into the business of custom shoemaking. So, at age 34, Jakob took his once-in-a-lifetime risk—his version of crossing the Carpathian Mountains—he would set up shop in America. In January, 1909, Jakob bade farewell to his wife and four children, and journeyed to Minneapolis where he had a sister and successful brother-in-law, Sussy and Herman Kliffer, with whom he could stay until he had raised enough money to bring the rest of the family over. The change of venue did little to improve Jakob's work habits. He loafed in America, and took three years to put together enough money to buy five tickets for sea passage.

With Jakob gone, Gitel managed the family in Romania. Illiterate and deeply religious, even superstitious, she told the children terrifying stories about the persecution of Jews that had begun in ancient times and continued in the pogroms of the late 1800s and early 1900s. Two particularly horrific pogroms had taken place in the nearby Ukrainian towns of Kishinev, in 1903, and Odessa, in 1905. Danger, hatred and anti-Semitic behavior lurked much closer to home as well. A neighbor shouted obscenities against Jews, schoolyard bullies beat them up. Joe Juran's most vivid recollection of his life in Gurahumora is of an "all-pervasive fear."

Townspeople called Joe "spider" because he was so small and wiry. One day, while rambling in the foothills, he slipped on a wet plank and dislocated his hip. Passersby carried him to a hut inhabited by a hermit who had some knowledge of bone setting. But, without traction, Joe ended up with a shortened leg which, in conjunction with a kink in the spine (possibly from scoliosis), left him with an uneven gait. On another ramble in the hills, Joe came across a hideous and unforgettable sight: A man had hanged himself from a tree and there he dangled, his oxygen-starved tongue sticking out, rigid and blue.

Joe may have been fearful; he was also extremely bright. He attended the village Hebrew school, where they spoke Yiddish, and the Gurahumora public school, where classes were conducted in German. Joe caused a commotion in the Jewish community when he taught himself to read Rashi, a form of ancient Hebrew text written, in large part, without vowels. People thought: Perhaps Joe will be a scholar, even a rabbi. But Joe viewed Rashi as an intriguing code, a secret writing, something to be deciphered. He would be attracted by the mystery of codes, linguistic challenges, and puzzles throughout his life—learning English, studying cryptanalysis in the Signal Corps, and working as an industrial problem solver.

Finally, the tickets for passage aboard the ship *Mount Temple* arrived from Jakob, along with a delightful novelty, a calendar in English. The kids—Rudy (11), Rebecca (9), Joe (7), and Nat (5)—delighted in pronouncing the abbreviations for the days of the week, MON, TUES, WED. On their day of departure from Gurahumora, it seemed to Joe that the whole town turned out at the train station to bid the family good-bye. He saw that his mother had the respect of the village. The train chugged north into Ukraine, across Poland and finally to the seaport of Antwerp, Belgium.

In August 1912, the Jurans boarded the ship *Mount Temple,* with some trepidation: the *Titanic* had sunk in April of that year. Their tickets were for steerage, where women and children slept on bunks—stacked three and four high—on one side of the ship, and men slept on the other. When Joe got the top bunk, he was wary of the scalding steam pipes that clanged and sputtered just overhead. Despite the dangers and discomforts, Juran remembers the voyage to America as "a big adventure." The ship docked at Quebec City, Quebec—east of Montreal, on the St. Lawrence River—on August 19, 1912 (see Figure 1.2). Atop the sharply rising cliffs stood the Chateau Frontenac, a hotel so grand it looked like a palace. A great railroad bridge spanned the river above the city. With most of their cash exhausted, the Jurans

Figure 1.2 The Jurans arrived in Quebec City on August 19, 1912, then traveled by train to Minneapolis.

stayed a few days in a hotel, until more money arrived. There, they experienced for the first time some of the supreme delights of a technological society—flush toilets and ice cream.

When the money came, they continued their journey by third-class rail to Sault Ste. Marie, Michigan. They crossed the border into the United States on August 22, and continued west to Minneapolis. Aboard the train, Gitel bought an exotic piece of fruit—a banana—for the children to try, but they couldn't figure out how to eat it. Finally, another passenger suggested they peel it, and everyone enjoyed a taste.

In Minneapolis, Jakob's sister met them at the station and helped them onto the Central Avenue streetcar, another novelty, which carried them out to their new home at the very outskirts of the city. A tarpaper shack.

New World Hardships

Although Minneapolis was a burgeoning Mississippi River town, busy with flour-milling and lumber production, Jakob had not found a way to contribute to or participate in its prosperity. Rather than set up his own shoemaking shop, he'd taken a job as a cobbler, at $9 a week. He liked to sleep late, smoke hand-rolled cigarettes, drink coffee, and play pinochle with his newfound cronies.

He had managed to secure a lot—apart from the Jewish community—on Central Avenue, then surrounded by woods and fields, now part of central Minneapolis. There he built a shack, measuring 12 by 30 feet, where the six Jurans now lived—just as they had in Gurahumora—without electricity, gas, indoor plumbing, or central heat. The ate their meals in the kitchen, warmed by the wood-burning stove. All the children—who soon totaled six (two more daughters, Minerva and Charlotte, were born in America)—slept together in the middle room. Jakob and Gitel slept in the front parlor. And Jakob's pal Nikolai would often scale the ladder at the end of the house for a snooze in the loft. Behind the shack stood a shed and, behind it, the outhouse, which "buzzed with flies in the summer and whistled up icy drafts in the winter," according to Joe's brother Nat. Streetcars thundered back and forth, yards from the front door.

In the fall of 1912, Rudy, Joe, and Nat reported to the Prescott School on Lowry Avenue, about a mile away. All were assigned to the first grade until they could be evaluated. Soon enough, Joe was catapulted from the first grade to the fourth. Although proud of his ascendancy, Joe now found himself as not only the smallest person in his class, but the youngest as well—a natural target for school bullies. To make matters more difficult, the Juran boys at first spoke only German. With a war brewing in Europe, they were identified with the enemy. "When school let out for a recess and we stepped out the door, here were all these kids saying, 'Charge the enemy!'," wrote Nat. "If we could outrun them, we were safe. If not, we got a beating." They learned English quickly.

For all its perils, school also brought rewards. Joe was pleased to be the youngest and smartest in his class, he loved to read, and he excelled at math and science. But his life in Minneapolis was dominated by work. During the school year, Joe worked mornings before school, after school until dinner, and on weekends. Summers, he worked full time. His first job, in the fall of 1912, was selling newspapers. Every morning except Sunday, he and Rudy would get up early to divide a big bundle of the Minneapolis *Tribune* that had been dropped outside their door. Rudy lugged his papers up to the 37th Street streetcar stop, Joe took his down to 33rd Street. At a penny a copy, they grossed about forty cents on a sellout day. They split the money with the company, and every penny the boys earned went straight to their father. No allowance. No pocket money. When the *Tribune* raised its price to two cents, the Jurans' profits did not rise with it. Joe thought it was unfair, but he said nothing about it.

As poor as they were, the Juran children did not feel particularly disadvantaged. Everybody else they knew was poor, too. When the kids weren't at school or working, they worked at home. They cut and split firewood for the stove, tended the vegetable garden, fed the chickens, and scoured the railroad tracks for lumps of coal to burn in the stove. In winter, they crawled underneath the shack and, with a hatchet, hacked out hunks of frozen sauerkraut from the barrel stored there. They ran to the butcher for unsalable bits of offal and organs. The children liked brains and liver pretty well, but the animals' stomach and lung coated the child's mouth with fat and often resulted in a bout of diarrhea.

Gitel worked constantly to keep her children healthy and prospering. She jarred pickles and preserves. She baked bread and, sometimes, an apple strudel. Most often, she fed the children a hot cornmeal mush served with cold milk called mummaliga. "To this day, it haunts my taste buds," Nat wrote later.

Even with school and work, the kids found time for fun. In the winter, they tobogganed on a curled-up sheet of corrugated metal; in summer, they picked wild strawberries and blueberries, and played baseball in the field across the street. Joe preferred indoor games, particularly checkers. Rudy and Nat seldom wanted to challenge him, however, because he was virtually unbeatable. There were no movies, no family vacations, no meals out. No kids were allowed to visit after school. No adults came to call.

Joe's next job was at Walker's grocery store, just off Central Avenue. O.J. Walker had noticed the enterprising immigrant kid hawking newspapers at the corner near his shop, and figured he'd make a good clerk. In the summer of 1913, Walker hired Joe at a dollar a week—for three hours after school and half a day on Saturdays—to man the cash register, tend the soda fountain, grind coffee, and manage the inventory of barrels of pickles, sacks of sugar and flour, soap, spices, and snuff. There were dozens of prices to memorize, but in those days Joe had what he calls a "flypaper memory." He never twice asked Mr. Walker to tell him a price. He did all the sales calculations in his head, not deigning to use the printed card perched on the cash register, where prices and units were displayed in an easy-to-read grid.

At age 11, Juran went to work keeping the books for Pete Corbin, who operated an ice house. Joe knew next to nothing about accounting or double-entry bookkeeping, but he was a faster learner than Corbin and had soon established a system for keeping track of how much ice had gone out and how much had been paid for. The system provoked some grumbling from the delivery men, who were now required to keep better records than they had before Juran's arrival— an early taste of what came to be called "cultural resistance." In the summer, when Corbin's team of horses was not hauling ice, they pulled a water tank that sprinkled the city streets to keep the dust down. Spidery Joe Juran drove the team of big horses, stopping every mile or so to fill the tank from a hydrant.

From age 12 to age 16, Juran held more jobs than most people hold in a lifetime. He worked as a packer, an errand boy, an office boy, a shipping clerk, a bundle boy, a shoe salesman, a house wrecker, and a printer's helper. Most jobs were, to him, just jobs. But when he interviewed for a job as a shoe salesman at a discount retail operation called M. W. Savage, he was surprised to find that they were interested in his education. "The fact that I was a high school student and that I was also ahead in my grades made a good impression. That struck me."

Both parents valued education. Gitel, who had no schooling at all, placed educated people, particularly doctors, on a pedestal. Even Jakob, who had abandoned his own studies, believed strongly in education and offered a dollar—at that time, a substantial amount—to any of his children who brought home a report card with all A's. Only Joe won the dollar, but his work schedule kept him from being the student he might have been. Although he did well in math, science, languages, and English, he often found himself bored. "I was way ahead of the other youngsters. I didn't study. And being bored, I began to get into childish pranks that had no place in the classroom and that depressed some of my grades."

But Juran read widely: Jack London, O. Henry, Greek and Scandinavian mythology. And he played with mathematical problems. In his sophomore year, he discovered—or reinvented—the figure known as a magic square (see Figure 1.3), an arrangement of nine

Figure 1.3 The magic square.

2	9	4
7	5	3
6	1	8

single digits placed within a grid so that any three of them added in any order—horizontally, vertically, or diagonally—yields the sum of fifteen.

Juran studied and worried the numbers until he derived a formula for constructing the square that worked every time. This seemed to him an amazing discovery, a universal. He found that he loved algebra, in general. "I discovered a formula that 2x plus 3x equals 5x, no matter whether you're talking about acorns or kids or anything else. So I was sensitized to this idea of universals way back." Juran often refers to his lifework as a search for the "underlying principles" or "universals" of business management, and the pursuit seems to have had its roots in this early joy at the reliability and predictability of algebraic formulas.

In Joe's sophomore year of high school, 1917, the Jurans moved to a new house, resplendent with flush toilets and running water, and, around 1919, the family fortunes picked up a little, thanks to a new source of income for Jakob—bootlegging. But in the spring of the following year, just as life had begun to show some prosperity, Gitel fell ill. The doctors diagnosed tuberculosis and admitted her to a sanitarium. That June, Joe graduated from high school, one of 20 honor students in a class of 226. On one of his visits to his mother, he realized that she was dying. "Neither of us said a word. But a great deal of feeling was conveyed. I knew she was dying. She knew she was dying. But I doubt she was commiserating with herself about what a horrible life she had led. I suspect this feeling—the warmth, the love she had for her children, was enough."

Juran not only idealizes his mother, he considers her to be as close to a role model as any person in his life, "in terms of humanity, integrity, unselfishness." He remembers how, on blizzard days, she would come to school, envelop her children under a blanket thrown round her shoulders, and shepherd them home as they clung to her dress, protected from the storm. On one particularly fierce day, Joe remembers that his mother walked the mile to school, then presented him with a nickel to take the streetcar home, while she walked.

Gitel died September 4, 1920, just as Joe went off to the University of Minnesota—the first Juran to attend college. The family soon disintegrated. Rudy, the oldest, was already on his own. Rebecca married. Jakob placed the little girls, Minerva (7) and Charlotte (5), in an orphanage. Joe and Nat moved with their father into a dingy, rat-infested duplex apartment at 2823 Grand Avenue South, in Minneapolis.

Juran had reached his fifteenth year with what he later came to regard as a "grudge against the world." To him, the world seemed a mean and hostile place, populated with school bullies, anti-Semites, and a pantheon of petty tyrants, including his father and his many employers. Worse, he had to put up with a world full of people whose minds were less quick than his own. He was physically small, and, culturally, an outsider. His mother, the one person whom he cherished and trusted, had died at the age of 39.

THE FIRST JURAN AT UNIVERSITY

On the suggestion of his high school physics teacher, Juran entered the electrical engineering program at the University of Minnesota. He had no particular passion for engineering, but had always been skilled at math and science, so the choice made sense. He was a young freshman, only 15, thanks to his late birthday (December 24) and having skipped two grades ahead in elementary school. From his father's apartment, Joe could take the streetcar downtown to the University mall—the stately buildings lining a greensward that gently descends to the Mississippi—or he could walk. Most days he walked, to save the five cent fare.

Juran was an able student, but not a standout. He might have achieved better grades, but two factors intervened. One was work, which continued to consume most of his nonclass hours. Tuition, after all, stood at $25 per semester. The other factor, which Juran had not anticipated, was chess. Early in his freshman year, a neighbor named Soderburg had introduced Juran to chess. The boy who had cracked the Rashi code and who had dominated his brothers at checkers, took to the game immediately. Within weeks, he had outstripped Soderburg's abilities. At home, he challenged his brother Nat to play while they lay in bed, after lights-out. "We'd play chess just by visualizing the board and calling out the moves," Nat laughs. "But after maybe six or eight moves, I'd be lost. But Joe knew exactly where every piece was, so he always won."

Juran had found his best game, an ideal application for his mental skills. Chess demands a great deal of analysis, which has to be accomplished quickly. Juran explains that "speed is one of the big elements in chess. The top chess player can mentally run through many more combinations in a very short time than his competitors, although many people don't realize that. They see players sitting there and nobody's moving and cobwebs are starting to collect—it looks like an awfully dull game. But if they could watch the pieces move as fast as they're being visualized by the players, they'd just see a blur."

Joe joined the Chess and Checkers Club at the university and, in his sophomore year, took the university chess championship, which he successfully defended through graduation. "That was a tremendous thing to me," he remembers. The title brought him status and recognition, not only with his classmates, but with the faculty as well. But, like his father with pinochle, Juran became consumed with chess. It distracted him from his studies and precluded other campus activities. He went on only one date in his entire college career.

Joe continued to live with his father, who spent much of his time at the shoe repair shop with his cronies Peegust and Heisel, Bayer and Goldsahn, and the former loft-snoozer, Nikolai. In air blue with smoke, Jakob talked politics, declaring his support for Eugene V. Debs, the Socialist Party candidate for president in 1920 (not to mention 1900, 1904, 1908, and 1912). Joe found a formula that enabled him to steer clear of his father's irascibility. "Joe was interested in studying and improving his mind," recalls Nat, "so he never got into much trouble" with Jakob. "Joe seemed to avoid all that. He was too smart."

Nathan, however, got into plenty of trouble. In his freshman year of high school, Nat was invited to his first party. Jakob allowed him to go, if he would promise to get home by 10 P.M. But the party was fun, the kids got to singing around the piano, and Nat lost track of time. At 11:00, he called home in a panic. Joe answered the phone. Nat said, "Tell Pa I'm coming right home." Joe relayed the message to his father, who replied, "Don't bother. Tell him to come tomorrow and get his stuff." Nat saw his father only once after that. "A few years later, I was working in a fruit store, polishing the fruit out front. He walked by and said hello and I said hello. And he said, 'How are you doing?' And I said, 'I'm doing fine.' And he said, 'Do you have your money for school and so on?' I pulled out my bankbook and showed him my balance. And that was it. He took off and I never saw him again. He was a disciplinarian. A hard man."

Joe continued to work at a variety of jobs throughout his university years. In the summer of 1922, however, he couldn't find any good work. The country had been in recession; there was labor unrest. He began to worry that he would not earn enough money to pay tuition the coming schoolyear. Then the shop men for the C.B.&Q. Railroad went on strike and Juran was offered a job changing locomotive brake shoes. He agonized over his unpleasant options: reject the job and lose out on his education, or work as a scab and earn the necessary tuition. He took the job, to his continuing regret.

In his junior year, Juran found a far more appealing—and lucrative—method of making money. The chess champion served as editor of a chess column for the Minneapolis *Daily Star* at the fantastic salary of $5 a week. It was his first experience with publishing.

In 1923, Juran did involve himself in a nonchess activity, the Reserve Officers Training Corps (ROTC) at the university. A major enticement for joining was the free uniforms the service offered, which could significantly reduce his wardrobe expenditure. Because he was an engineering student, he ended up in the Signal Corps, which was just getting involved in the newly emerging radio communications. In the Signal Corps, Juran found a new fascination: cryptanalysis, the deciphering of coded messages. After being commissioned in the Signal Corps Reserve in 1925, he served three five-year hitches.

RECRUITMENT

In the spring of 1924, Juran faced the questions all graduating college seniors face: What shall I do next? How shall I make my way in the world? For whom shall I work? He had no intention of continuing his education. His goal was to find a steady job at steady pay. In early March, representatives of several large corporations visited the University of Minnesota campus. Recruitment on campus was a relatively new phenomenon. Western Electric Company, a subsidiary of American Telephone & Telegraph Company (AT&T), had begun its program of recruitment in 1910, but had only begun advertising in campus publications in 1921.

From his interviews, Juran received three job offers—from the General Electric Company, Western Union, and Western Electric. Rumor had it that, although General Electric was a highly-regarded company, the college recruit generally would start out on the test floor at the company's huge plant in Schenectady, New York, and advancement could be difficult. The people from Western Union were pleasant enough, but the telegraph business seemed pretty stodgy, especially in comparison to the telephone industry. Besides, in order to gain a rise in salary at Western Union, it was necessary to have skill in the operation of a telegraph key. To 19-year-old chess champion Joe Juran, this did not sound like a "noble job. I think they didn't put their best foot forward, and maybe they didn't have a best foot to put forward."

So, Juran accepted the offer from Western Electric. He was to report to work at their Hawthorne Works facility in Chicago, one of the largest industrial plants in the world. He would receive the standard starting salary of $27 for a week's work, which included a half day on Saturday.

At first, Juran had little, if any, idea of what a perspicacious choice he had made. On his first day of work, he joined his fellow college recruits in an indoctrination program, after which the indoctrinees were dealt out to the various departments, almost at random, it seemed. Juran found himself in something called The Inspection Branch. "I wasn't very clear on what they did. I didn't care. I didn't have any idea that here's something that's going to be a major concern of society."

2

The Big Ship Hawthorne

(1920–1941)

No factory in the world could compete with Hawthorne in the majesty of its design.

Ronald Pook
Hawthorne historian

THE GREAT FACTORIES

Juran began his career—and paid his professional dues—on the manufacturing floor of a factory that has attained a legendary status in industrial history. Western Electric's Hawthorne Works, in addition to its primary role as manufacturer of equipment for AT&T, became a kind of working laboratory for inquiry into the emerging issues of the large industrial organization at the beginning of the twentieth century. What is the most effective organizational structure? What methods should we use to control the manufacturing quality of precision parts? How should we handle the human issues and problems that arise in an industrial culture?

W. Edwards Deming, too, worked at Hawthorne, during the summers of 1925 and 1926, while attaining his PhD at Yale. "On arrival on the fifth floor," Deming recalled, "Mr. Chester M. Coulter, whom I reported to, made it clear to me as most important—don't get caught on the stairway when the whistle blows. Those women would trample you to death: there would be no trace of you. There were 46,000 people that worked at the Hawthorne plant, and I think that 43,000 of them had high heels. I did not get caught." In actual fact, there were more like 43,000 people at Hawthorne (at its peak in the late 1920s), about 30 percent of whom were women. (The percentage of those who wore high heels is not known.) The young, spidery inspector Juran and the tall graduate student Deming did not come in contact at Hawthorne and did not meet until the World War II years.

Juran came to Hawthorne during the adolescence of the huge, vertically integrated factory. Most, if not all, ingredients and functions needed to create a product were owned or controlled by the producer. Industrial entrepreneurs, notably Henry Ford, played on a grand scale with assembling all the critical aspects of a manufacturing process under one virtual roof. Ford's River Rouge plant, for example, boasted both a steel plant and a glass factory as well as a wholly owned rubber plant in Brazil and iron mines in Minnesota. Hawthorne too, although smaller than Ford's industrial conurbation, was conceived and developed as a vertically integrated factory. Hawthorne resembled a small city, with 100 buildings sprawled across a site of nearly 200 acres. (Ford's River Rouge plant comprised 93 buildings on 1,100 acres, and employed 75,000 people.)

The Hawthorne Works included a rod-and-wire mill for drawing wire; a cable plant in which, each year, some 30 billion feet of copper wire were converted into sheathed cable and rolled onto great wooden reels; and a foundry to produce metal components. Hawthorne ran its own power plant, maintained a private fire brigade, and operated a private railroad, the Manufacturer's Junction Railway, complete with roundhouse and six miles of track, to transport raw materials and finished goods around the plant. In 1924, the year Juran arrived, the telephone apparatus group manufactured some 155,000 different components and assembled them into 12,000 different types of telephones and apparatus products.

As factories like Hawthorne expanded, as if their owners wished to create a complete world within the bounding walls, a new structure for the owner-operator corporations emerged. After World War I, the national economy had dipped into a recession, and the big industrial organizations experienced a weak market for the first time in their young lives. Alfred Chandler, the business historian, writes, "The sharp recession following World War I had a shattering impact on many of the new industrial and marketing companies. The majority had been established after the depression of the 1890s. The sudden and continuing drop in demand from the summer of 1920 until the spring of 1922 was, therefore, the first period of hard times that the modern business enterprise had to face."

Alfred P. Sloan, Jr., who in 1920 was a member of the executive committee of General Motors, recalls: "The automobile market had nearly vanished and with it our income. Most of our plants and those of the industry were shut down or assembling a small number of cars out of semifinished materials in the plants. We were loaded with high-priced inventory and commitments at the old inflated price level. We were short of cash. We had a confused product line. There was a lack of control and of any means of control in operations and finance, and a lack of adequate information about anything. In short, there was just about as much crisis, inside and outside, as you could wish for if you liked that sort of thing."

This crisis led to a realization that no company could count on a constantly rising market, and that some method of planning activities, making purchases based on projected need, and adjusting production to meet actual demand (by studying current sales results) had to be implemented. In 1920, Sloan proposed for General Motors an organizational structure of "decentralized operations with coordinated control" that would be "a happy medium in industrial organization between the extremes of pure centralization and pure decentralization." This is the structure we are so familiar with today, in which a centralized administrative body consisting of a number of discipline-based departments (engineering, accounting, and so on) sets policy, coordinates, and controls the actions of a number of decentralized and largely autonomous operating divisions. Lines of authority are clearly defined in a tiered hierarchy that resembles a pyramid. The ranks of each ascending tier grow less and less populous and more and more powerful, and the ultimate power resides at the top.

For all its strengths, the inherent weaknesses of a Sloan-style organizational structure are that it fragments the central process (car making or telephone assembly), sharply defines responsibility and authority, and establishes barriers between disciplines. The new structure hastened the emergence of management as a profession and helped create a new class of businessperson known as the middle manager. In 1925, AT&T reorganized along the lines of the Sloan model, centralizing its research and planning functions in New York and redefining Western Electric as an operating unit, that was responsible for manufacturing but not for product design and development.

So, Juran came to Western Electric at a time of great excitement and change in the way business was conducted in America. The postwar recession had ended, a period of economic prosperity (under newly elected President Calvin Coolidge) had begun, and AT&T had assumed the basic shape it would hold for the next sixty years or so.

PRECISION IN CHAOS

In 1924, the telephone had been in existence for nearly 50 years. Some 12 million phones were in use in The Bell System, and Americans talked on the phone about 50 million times a day. The Bell Telephone network had grown into a complex system of phones, connecting wire and cable, switching apparatus, and transmission equipment. There were thousands of individual components; many were small and precise parts that had to run efficiently on small amounts of electricity. And, equally as important, all the components and products had to function together in one great network, a system that was constantly growing and evolving. What's more, the elements of the system had to function in a wide variety of environments and be maintainable by people with widely differing levels of skill.

"The Bell System was at that time facing some massive quality problems which its sister industries were not to face until decades later," writes Juran, "a bewilderingly complex system; unprecedented interchangeability of mechanical apparatus and electrical circuitry; extremely close tolerances of manufacture and measurement; severe requirements for reliability and maintainability." There was far more possibility of error and variation in the manufacture of telephone equipment than in the other major products of the day: textiles, ships, steel, locomotives, and agricultural machinery, or even in the production of electric engines and automobiles. As the sole supplier of telephone equipment to the burgeoning Bell System, the problem of ensuring quality fell squarely on the shoulders of Western Electric and its major plant, The Hawthorne Works.

Western Electric had been The Bell System's manufacturing partner since 1882, but had begun its life as a manufacturer of electrical equipment, including telegraph instruments, fire alarms, and signal boxes for Bell's archrival, Western Union. By 1900, Western Electric employed nearly 9,000 people, in two plants—one in downtown Chicago, the other in New York City. In 1903, the company purchased 163 acres of land in what was then a barren piece of prairie on the outskirts of Chicago, an area known as Hawthorne. Construction of the new facility began in 1904—the year of Juran's birth—and operations began in 1905.

Hawthorne, like many factories of the day, had been set up as a colony of specialist craft shops, rather like a town of individual entrepreneurs arranged along a village street, with the difference that these shops had to work together to create a single product or, at least, products that would function successfully in a larger system. Hawthorne had not adopted Ford's assembly line technique (which had gone into operation in 1913 at the Ford Highland Park plant). Rather, all the milling machines were grouped in one area and all the drill presses in another. Metal finishing was done in a separate area. Tapping machines were down the hall; assembly operations around the corner. "In the colony organization," recalls Juran, "if there was some component that required quite a few different operations, it had to thread its way in and out, up and down, and through all those factory departments. It took a long time to do that. It had to get moved there. It had to wait its turn. And then wait its turn before it was shipped to the next department. It might take weeks or even months before it finished that journey." With 155,000 components being made at Hawthorne, 12,000 products assembled, and 40,000 people hard at work, the quantities and confusion of criss-crossing materials, work in progress, parts, components, finished goods, people, and paperwork approached a state of constant chaos.

To tame the chaos, and to ensure that defective products did not go out the door, Hawthorne relied on the accepted quality assurance method of the day: inspection. To inspect all incoming material, work in progress, finished goods, and products in the field required an enormous operation. Western Electric employed 5,000 inspectors in its Inspection Branch—composed of a Shop Complaint Department and a Field Complaint Department—about one-eighth of the entire plant population. The responsibility of the Inspection Branch, Juran remembers, "was to separate good product from bad. The good product went on to the next stage or to the shipping department. The bad product went back to be discarded or repaired or whatever."

The priorities of inspectors and of the workers and line managers they inspected were different and often conflicting. Juran recalls: "The priorities for the production department were to meet their schedules and meet their productivity goals so that the workers could get good piece work pay. The priority of the Inspection Department was quality. And they enforced that priority by virtue of their command of the inspection stamps. Before anything could be moved from one place to another there had to be an inspection stamp on the identification document. And the Inspection Branch controlled those stamps and they saw to it that nothing would move unless it met their quality requirements."

Juran viewed the job as a delicious challenge. "It got me all over the place," says Juran. "I was a pretty bright youngster, I had a fabulous memory and I got to have an encyclopedic knowledge of what went on in that factory." The plant was riddled with problems of material, tools, equipment, procedures and operators, all of which threatened schedules or outgoing quality. Juran's problem-solving adventures amounted to an educating immersion in all aspects of manufacturing. He found that his analytical skills, which he had honed as a chess champion at the University of Minnesota, stood him in good stead at the factory. "In chess, there are a number of different modes. One is, you just play safe. Tighten up all the chinks in the armor and nothing can get through. Wait for the other guy to make a mistake. That's not the way I played. I would take a gamble. I'd give this away because I saw a means of attack and the other guy didn't. So, I won many games by that method. And translating that into a company like Western

Electric. People conferred with each other, 'What should we do in this situation?' There are lots of options open. If you could come up with an option that hadn't been thought of that is going to be agreed to by the powers that be, you've scored a kind of victory."

Juran's knowledge of the Hawthorne operations, combined with his analytical skills, youthful energy, ferocious capacity for work, and tremendous drive to succeed, caused him to question the prevailing inspection method early in his career. He realized that his activities provided only short-term fixes to short-term problems and had absolutely no effect on the system. The same problems would regularly recur and new problems would constantly arise. In his later writings, Juran liked to refer to this type of situation as a swamp full of alligators. No matter how many alligators you kill, new ones keep hatching and coming to get you.

One early assignment made a particularly strong impression on Juran. His boss sent him to investigate the production of a tiny circuit breaker. The inspectors were scrapping about 15 percent of the circuit breakers because they didn't meet the specification for electrical resistance. Working with the production supervisor, Juran went at the problem methodically, focusing on a key component of the circuit breaker, a wire-wound coil. Suspecting that the cause might be variation in the resistance of the wire itself, the two men cut identical lengths from a number of different supply reels and found that their suspicion was correct. To bring the resistance to specification, they compensated for the variance in resistance by adjusting the length of wire cut from each reel.

"To my surprise," wrote Juran, "the result was only a slight drop in the defect rate. We were still scrapping more than 10 percent of the product because it failed to meet the resistance specification." Next, Juran measured and plotted the resistance of the finished circuit breakers and found that although fairly uniform it was uncomfortably close to the minimum specification. Puzzled, Juran looked more closely at the manufacturing process itself. He found that the workers soldered the wire to the coil, not at the very tip of the wire, but at a point about two inches from the end, thus shortening the effective length of the wire and reducing its total resistance. Juran increased the specified length of wire by two inches, and the defect rate plummeted to near zero. He was "fascinated by the experience. We had analyzed the process to find the sources of our problems and then fixed them, which had the effect of increasing our production of these little circuit breakers by about 15 percent, without extra machines, extra people, or extra material. In other words, by improving the production process, we had not only improved the quality of the circuit breakers, we had also lowered the cost of producing them."

Juran, knowing that dozens of similar opportunities existed throughout the Works, excitedly proposed to his boss that he search them all out, fix them all, and realize tremendous savings and improvements. The boss "agreed that this would be a wonderful thing to do, but he said it wasn't our job. 'We're the Inspection Department,' I remember him saying, 'and our job is to look at these things after they're made and find the bad ones. Making them right in the first place is the job of the Production Department. They don't want us telling them how to do their job, just as we don't want them telling us how to do ours.' And that's where it ended."

The experience for Juran was a seminal one. He had faced and solved a chronic problem through a process of investigation and improvement that he could repeat, and he had realized cost reductions and quality improvements that were measurable and significant, and that required no capital investment. But he had been unable to apply his learnings more broadly, stymied by a rigid structure and the not-invented-here mentality it engendered.

SCIENTIFIC MANAGEMENT

Although Juran was only dimly aware of it at the time, the barriers he had crashed into had been deliberately erected and their construction had been recommended, in a general way, by the most influential management thinker of the day, Frederick Winslow Taylor. Taylor was deeply concerned about the practice of "soldiering" or "slow-working." Most men, he believed (and he always referred to workers as men, despite the fact that women had a major presence in manufacturing) did not work to their full capacity. He identified three key reasons for soldiering:

1. The workman believes that if he increases his individual output it will eventually lead to "throwing a large number of men out of work."
2. "Defective systems of management" make it necessary for men to soldier, in order to protect their own best interests.
3. "The inefficient rule-of-thumb methods, which are still almost universal in all trades, and in practicing them which our workmen waste a large part of their effort."

Taylor's solution—which came to be known as scientific management—was that "the management must take over and perform much of the work which is now left to the men; almost every act of the workman should be preceded by one or more preparatory acts of the management which enable him to do his work better and quicker than he otherwise could."

Taylor's idea was that work methods should be based on scientific study, rather than the "rule-of-thumb" methods used by craft workers and developed empirically over years of work. As Taylor put it, "in almost all of the mechanic arts the science which underlies each act of each workman is so great and amounts to so much that the workman who is best suited to actually doing the work is incapable of fully understanding this science, without the guidance and help of those who are working with him or over him, either through lack of education or through insufficient mental capacity."

To develop these methods required the separation of the *planning* of work from the *execution* of work. In other words, the thinking would be done by managers, the production by "the hands." The work would be systematically analyzed, generally by studying the amount of time and the number and nature of the motions required by workers to accomplish a given task. Then, based on the findings of such studies, the tasks would be designed for maximum efficiency—with specifications for the types of tools to be used, the steps to be followed, and the type of worker best suited to the task. Once selected, the workers would be carefully trained in their task and compensated based on their ability to produce the specified output within the specified allotment of time. Although this sounds highly authoritarian, Taylor saw the relationship of management and the workforce as a "close, intimate, personal cooperation"—not a rigid, impersonal, authoritarian structure.

Taylor's thinking, particularly as applied in the great mass production facilities such as auto factories, produced the idea that "the workers on the shop floor were simply interchangeable parts of the production system," as Womack, Jones, and Roos put it in *The Machine That Changed the World*. Taylor's ideas sound less outrageous today— we are used to hearing about the benefits of teamwork and the organizational joys of worker empowerment—when considered in context. The typical factory worker of the early decades of the twentieth century was poorly educated, by today's standards. As manufacture grew in complexity, that lack of education proved a serious detriment to the worker's ability to understand the concepts required to accomplish a job. Equally significant, a large percentage of the factory workers Taylor was describing were immigrants with little or no grasp of the English language. They literally could not understand instructions given to them. Hawthorne, for example, was its own melting pot of immigrants, from Czechoslovakia, Poland, Lithuania, Scandinavia, Italy, and elsewhere.

Taylor's principles of scientific management, which he first articulated in 1895, were intended to help business owners gain control over their costs so they could better weather the ups and downs in demand that plagued the growing factories. Hawthorne, in the 1920s, operated with a combination of the traditional craft organization, which Juran remembers, and scientific management. Each shop employed many operators who used rule-of-thumb techniques to get their machines to create parts that would meet specifications. Yet they did not create the specifications, nor did they control the entire process of creating any product (as would a traditional craftsman such as a shoemaker).

The Taylor system worked. "It achieved spectacular improvements in productivity," says Juran. "Under Taylor's competent advocacy, the system was widely adopted by American industry, took firm root and remains as the principal base on which our managerial structures have been erected. The Taylor system provided a strong impulse to the movement to separate inspection from production, i.e., to use full-time inspectors for product inspection and process control rather than to rely on the workmen."

So, at Hawthorne, Juran and his army of fellow inspectors were engaging in an ad hoc form of Taylorism—devising work plans to replace rule-of-thumb methods, but on a case-by-case basis and only when a problem arose. They were not able, or expected, to improve the system itself.

※

PERSONAL GOALS

In June 1924, days after graduation, Juran moved from Minneapolis to Chicago, where Hawthorne was located. Of his $27 weekly Western Electric salary, $4 a week went to rent a small room near the Works. After his other expenses—which, by most accounts, included very little for clothing—whatever was left went into his newly opened savings account at Pinkert State Bank.

With a good job and his own apartment, Juran soon began to contemplate a new goal: "acquiring a family," as he calls it. In the fall of 1924, Juran's older sister Rebecca came to Chicago to visit a girlhood friend, now living there. Juran went to the railway station to meet Rebecca, and there encountered the friend, Sadie Shapiro. It seems that one look was all that was required for Juran to determine that this was the woman who could help him achieve his latest goal. "Once I saw that slender hunk of pulchritude I was smitten," Juran wrote. "My courtship had more than a year to run, but any good observer could have written me off as a goner."

Sadie's impression of the spidery, poorly dressed, socially awkward Juran was different. "I went down to the Northwestern train station in Chicago to meet Rebecca, and there was her brother. He picked up her suitcase, and we got on the streetcar. And he seemed to be very—I don't know what word to use—he just couldn't take his eyes off me. In fact, he was so confused, he forgot to pay the fare until we got off."

At that time, Juran had had only one date with a girl, in his senior year at college. It wasn't long before he asked Sadie out. "I agreed to meet him at the Art Institute on Michigan Boulevard. We went through the museum. He took me out to dinner. He took me to the theater in the evening. And then he wanted me to go on a date with him every Saturday. And then, before long, he told me that he would like me not to make dates with anybody else."

Shapiro, at age 19, was not quite ready for such a controlled situation, and decided to cool things down by taking a job in Minneapolis for six months. Juran took up the pursuit through correspondence, however, and she finally agreed to marry. The wedding took place June 26, 1925, in Chicago. The Jurans moved into a small apartment on Madison Avenue, downtown. The name of their landlord— Dr. Levitt, a dentist—was painted on their living room window. Sadie's mother, who had initially disapproved of Juran, decided to move in with the newlyweds. Mrs. Juran worked for the first two years of their marriage, until their first son, Robert, was born, in January 1927. Juran had more than accomplished his personal goal. Not only had he acquired a family, he had acquired a mother-in-law, too.

GAINING CONTROL

Even with its army of eager young engineer-inspectors—including Juran—The Bell System was not satisfied with the quality of its manufactured products and set out to change its quality assurance methods. Beginning in 1882, Bell had inspected Western Electric's output. Theodore Vail had reorganized the system in 1907, and gave Western Electric the responsibility of inspecting its own products and ensuring that they met AT&T's standards. But the inspection methods Western Electric used were almost as rule-of-thumb as the production methods. The sampling methods were haphazard, with no statistical basis for the size of a sample or the frequency of a test. "There had been some degree of movement relative to use of statistical methods going back to the turn of the century," says Juran. "But generally they were volunteer efforts by people that got themselves interested and the like. Not so much an effort that was the result of a positive line of thinking by upper management."

As The Bell System grew in size, complexity and sophistication, Bell became concerned about relying too much on Western Electric for self-inspection with seat-of-the-pants methods. In 1922, AT&T introduced a new central office switching device, which brought the issue to a head. Bell piled on more inspectors to oversee field installation of the complicated new switches, but often wound up with more inspectors on the job than installers.

To help solve such problems, the company reorganized again in 1925. A separate research entity, Bell Telephone Laboratories (Bell Labs) was created from what had been the Western Electric Engineering Department, based in New York City. Bell Labs sprang into existence with 3,600 employees and a budget of $12 million. It was the largest of the industrial research labs of its day; the other key ones were run by General Electric, Kodak, and Du Pont. As one observer puts it, "The Bell System was now engaged in the manufacture of science, as well as telephones." Now that they were separated from Hawthorne, the Bell Labs staff began to consider the issue of quality in a more rigorous way. They sought to develop a mathematically-oriented theory of sampling and inspection, methods for stating quality, and economic standards of quality.

VARIATION

A major focus of research at Bell Labs was the subject of how best to reduce manufacturing variation. Reducing variation would have a direct impact on the defect rate at Hawthorne—then running as high as 20 percent—which would help reduce costs, improve productivity and quality, and reduce failures in the field.

Dr. Walter A. Shewhart, a former professor of physics, had joined the engineering department at Western Electric in 1918, and made the transition to research engineer and statistician when Bell Labs was formed in 1925. In May 1924, Dr. Shewhart described a new device that he thought might help with controlling manufacturing quality. Shewhart's boss at the time, George D. Edwards, recalled, "Dr. Shewhart prepared a little memorandum only about a page in length. About a third of that page was given over to a simple diagram which we would all recognize today as a schematic control chart. That diagram, and the short text which preceded and followed it, set forth all of the essential principles and considerations which are involved in what we know today as process quality control."

The idea of the control chart is wonderfully simple and seemingly obvious. "It is well known that nothing repeats itself precisely," explains Juran, "whether monthly sales, hourly production on the assembly line, or dimensions of pieces turned out by a lathe. This 'natural' fluctuation is the result of the interplay of numerous small variables and is called random or chance fluctuation, i.e. not traceable to any specific cause." Shewhart, in a paper written in 1926, referred to these as "non-assignable causes."

These small, random—nonassignable—variations affect any manufacturing facility and every manufactured product, in fact, anything that humans (or nature, for that matter) create. Shewhart provides the simplest of examples. "Write the letter *a* on a piece of paper," he writes. "Now make another *a* just like the first one; then another and another until you have a series of *a's, a, a, a, a, a, a.* You try to make all the *a's* alike, but you don't; you can't. You are willing to accept this as an empirically established fact."

The same is true of any manufactured part or component. In the manufacture of a milled metal part, for example, its dimensions will vary slightly from piece to piece, from batch to batch, because of thousands of variables including machine speed, variations in electrical current, the weather, time of day, differences in raw material, condition of machine components, machine settings, differences in the materials used in processing—such as fluxes or lubricants or cleaners, etc.—and on and on and on. These are random variations and they are inherent in any system for producing product, whether it's a person's hand creating *a's,* a machine stamping plastic parts, or a factory turning out assembled cars. Practically speaking, it might be impossible to remove these small fluctuations from a process; it certainly might not be cost-effective.

But there is another type of variation, one that occurs when the process runs way out of whack, failing to function at all or spitting out product that can only be scrapped or is very expensive to rework or fix. The annals of manufacturing are bursting with cases of this type of variation, which has come to be called "special variation." A special variation generally derives from what Shewhart called "assignable" causes and can be discovered and eliminated. "The reason for trying to find assignable causes is obvious," writes Shewhart, "it is only through the control of such factors that we are able to improve the product without changing the whole manufacturing process. But it would be a waste of time to try to ferret out or assign some cause for a fluctuation in product which is no greater than that which could have resulted from the non-assignable causes." In other words, the question for a manufacturing operation such as Hawthorne is to determine about any variation, as Juran puts it, "How big is big?" A "test of significance" is required. "Over the last few centuries," Juran writes, "mathematicians have learned how to calculate probabilities with various sizes of fluctuations, and have refined the tests of significance. But the effort to calculate and recalculate the probabilities was forbidding except in isolated cases."

Shewhart's control chart (see Figure 2.1) provided what Juran calls "a convenient, perpetual test of significance. The probabilities are calculated once, and a pair of horizontal boundary lines ('limit lines') are drawn to show the range of fluctuation which could be due to random causes alone. Then the actual performance (lot by lot, hour by hour, machine by machine, or whatever) is plotted on the chart. Points outside the limit lines are almost certainly due to findable causes."

Shewhart theorized that these special variations could be discovered through rigorous diagnosis, and could be corrected economically without making any fundamental changes to the system. In other words, the amount of money saved by removing the variation would be greater than the cost of discovering and remedying it.

Figure 2.1 An example of Shewhart's Control Chart. Dotted lines represent control limits. Points outside the lines represent special variation.

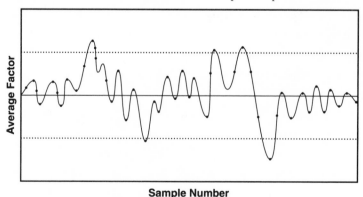

Sample Number

After special variations have been removed and the process is running with only what has been determined to be standard—or random—variation, it is said to be operating in "statistical control." Operating in statistical control means that the process will create components that consistently meet established specifications, but the random variation will continue as long as the process remains unchanged. Then the challenge becomes to narrow the upper and lower limits, so that the product or component is more and more consistent, closer and closer to "perfect." To do that generally requires a fundamental change to the system, a breakthrough. What to change and how to change it may require significant research, analysis, discussion, brainstorming, trial and error, fine-tuning, and so on.

These two aspects of manufacturing—control and breakthrough—as they were just coming to be understood at Hawthorne in the 1920s would form the basis of Juran's lifework.

THE EXPERTS TOUR THE FLOOR

In 1926, a team from Bell Labs—including Shewhart—visited Hawthorne to explore the possible application of their ideas for gaining better control of the manufacturing operations, including the control chart. In June, a Special Committee on Inspection Statistics and Economy was established. Six members were from Bell Labs, including George Edwards, Shewhart, Donald A. Quarles, and Harold Dodge; six members from the Inspection Development Branch at Western Electric; and five members from the Manufacturing Department of the Inspection Branch, including Juran. In addition, a professor of statistics from the University of Chicago, Walter Bartky, was brought in to provide the plant people with a crash course on statistical analysis.

Juran was assigned the job of piloting Shewhart around Hawthorne. Shewhart was 35 at the time, Juran was 21. Shewhart held a

PhD in Physics from the University of California, Berkeley. Juran held a BS in electrical engineering from the University of Minnesota. Shewhart, according to many who worked with him, had the air of the scholar about him. The statistician, said Juran, presented "the image of a theorist, exhibiting some flashes of brilliance, but mainly impractical and unintelligible." One can imagine Juran's managers, and probably Juran himself, watching Shewhart for any sign of incompetence or foolishness—as insiders will do when any outside expert comes to call. "He had never really been in a factory before," Juran remembers. "With respect to understanding of factory operations, his ignorance was complete. But with respect to some of the statistical tools, he was marvelous. He was a conceptualizer. That control chart is a delightful device. None of us would have minded inventing that thing."

The Special Committee, encouraged by their initial work, recommended that a new department be established at Hawthorne: an Inspection Statistical Department, probably the first of its kind in the United States. C.A. Melsheimer was the boss, commanding two young engineers, one of whom was Joseph Juran. Over the next three years, their task was to work with the Special Committee in developing ways to improve quality. But, in those early years, Shewhart's control chart "did not take at all," Juran says. "It is a sensitive detector of change and there was no need for that. If you have a machine and smoke is starting to come out of it, you don't need a sensitive thermometer to tell you this is heating up." In fact, Shewhart's control chart did not come into wider use until World War II; even then it continued to meet resistance and lack of understanding from manufacturing managers and line workers. Together, the team members explored a variety of new methods for assessing and controlling product and process quality, including sampling. Juran became so immersed and expert in the subject that, in 1928, he wrote his first pamphlet—*Statistical Methods Applied to Manufacturing Problems*—and designed a training course for Hawthorne's night school.

But statistical methods and tools could not provide a complete solution. "To me, the main contribution of these pioneers was not the control charts, the sampling tables, the rating plans, and the valuable rest. The main contribution was not even in the idea of statistical tools generally. Rather, the main contribution was, in my opinion, the fact that they were able to detach themselves from long-standing tradition sufficiently to re-examine some premises which had come to be regarded as axiomatic. Through this re-examination, they challenged some defective premises."

So, although Juran learned statistical methods and applied them in his work, the real significance of his collaboration with Shewhart and the Bell Labs team was that Juran—at age 21—began to understand that every plant operates in accordance with deep-seated assumptions and long-standing practices that may or may not be as productive or efficient as they could or should be. In short, he gained some support for his belief that Hawthorne—and, by inference, every industrial organization—can be improved. And he saw that the people most able to recognize the assumptions of an organization were observers who did not function within the system. They were outsiders, consultants.

Long before he actually became a consultant himself (in 1945), Juran got the idea that he might be able to peddle his services to other factories in the Chicago area that had conditions similar to Hawthorne's. Chicago, in the 1920s, was, in fact, a center of the growing business of consultancy. Arthur Andersen, McKinsey & Company, and Booz, Allen were all founded in Chicago and began to flourish in the 1920s. But, still content aboard the big ship Hawthorne, Juran did not act on his early inclinations toward the freelance life.

THE HUMAN FACTORS

Another type of outside observer came to study Hawthorne in the 1920s: academics with an interest in large manufacturing organizations, not for their processes and products, but as intriguing examples of a specialized type of human society. Throughout the 1920s,

Hawthorne was on a hiring binge, taking on new employees at the rate of 300 each month, many of them immigrants like Juran. The factory grew from 6,000 employees in 1919 to a peak of some 43,000 in 1929–1930, a sevenfold increase in 10 years.

Outside observers tended to view Hawthorne as a model factory. One foreign observer called it a "workers' paradise." In the opinion of Professor Elton Mayo, who conducted a series of experiments at Hawthorne that involved the human issues in what he called an industrial civilization, "The Western Electric Company would stand very high in a list of industrial institutions if the order in such a list were determined by consideration of the worker and a real concern for his welfare. In respect of hours of work and wages the Company stands above its compeers."

Indeed, Hawthorne offered benefits unknown in other companies and the amenities of a progressive, midsize town. In 1906, Western Electric had established the first pension plan. By the mid-1920s, another plan enabled employees to purchase AT&T stock at a discount. "This was introduced at Hawthorne by a mild mannered gentleman from headquarters," recounts the Hawthorne publication, *Microphone*. "He explained that it was all very simple—just a matter of arithmetic. All an office boy had to do was to start buying his quota every year and with no effort, retire with a very fancy bankroll. Since these were the days before Social Security, this was heady stuff."

There was a savings and loan institution, a laundry, a hospital (with a squadron of nurses who would make house calls), a park (complete with flower gardens, fountain, and bandshell), a gymnasium, and an athletic field with six baseball diamonds, thirteen tennis courts, and a running track. There was a Hawthorne baseball league and a women's basketball team known as The Ruthless Babes. Anyone could enroll in evening classes on dozens of subjects and participate in any number of clubs.

And yet, like many of the workers in the large factories of the time, Hawthorne men and women—especially recent immigrants— viewed the work as a stepping stone to a better job, or to starting their own small business. Few intended to make a career at Hawthorne; the line worker probably felt little loyalty to Western Electric. This attitude was demonstrated clearly in the rush for the stairs at shift-end, which Deming had recalled.

It wasn't until later, when the worker began to imagine factory work as the occupation of a lifetime—primarily due to increasing wage levels, such as Ford's astonishing $5 a day—that they began to see the shortcomings of the factory more clearly. Writing about workers in the Ford plants, Womack et al. write, "Eventually they began to stop dreaming about a return to the farm or to the old country and realize that a job at Ford was likely to be their life's work. When that realization dawned, their conditions of employment rapidly came to seem less and less bearable."

And, of course, underlying Hawthorne management's blandishments and benefits was a strong desire to prevent the workers from unionizing. Management succeeded until the passage of the National Labor Relations Act in 1935 (commonly known as the Wagner Act), which prohibited employers from interfering with the right of workers to unionize. In 1936, the 16,000 unskilled workers at Hawthorne formed a union and elected one Charlie Flax as its leader. "He had no apparent following, no apparent skills and less charm of manner," according to Ronald Pook, a Western Electric amateur historian.

THE ILLUMINATION STUDIES

Unionization was just one manifestation of the complex human issues involved in the operation of large factories such as Hawthorne, and social scientists became intrigued by them. The most famous studies of the "industrial civilization" of that era—and perhaps the most famous evaluations on the effect of human factors of any industrial endeavor—began as experiments to measure the effects of illumination on worker performance. These studies, not surprisingly, had their genesis in a business problem, rather than an altruistic inquiry into the well being of workers.

In 1913, a patent was granted for a process to produce tungsten filaments for use in electric lamps. Lamps with tungsten filaments shed considerably more and whiter light per watt than lamps made with the other materials used at the time, such as carbon. This worried the electricity generating companies; they feared that the electrical consumption, particularly of their large customers, would decrease and, along with it, their profits. So, in 1923, The General Electric Company provided funding for a series of tests by the Committee on Industrial Lighting—which was contained within the National Research Council of the National Academy of Science—to determine the relationship between the quality and quantity of illumination in the workplace and the efficiency and morale of the workers. The favored theory of the electricity providers was that increased illumination would lead to higher worker productivity, and, therefore, greater electricity usage and higher sales for them.

A team of researchers, led initially by Professor Dugald C. Jackson of the Electrical Engineering Department at the Massachusetts Institute of Technology, conducted a series of experiments in which they increased and decreased illumination with several groups of workers, and observed the effects. According to a synopsis of the studies, published by Western Electric, the effect was "puzzling":

> Output bobbed up and down in some groups or increased continually in others, or increased and stayed level in still others. But in no case was the increase or decrease in proportion to the increase or decrease in illumination. Where a parallel "control" group was set up for comparison with the test group undergoing changes in lighting, the production of the control group increased about the same as that of the test group.

The researchers, baffled, tried a different approach. They set up two groups of coil winders in an area of the plant that received no daylight, so that all the illumination would come from artificial light, which the researchers could completely control and manipulate. A control group worked under a constant, comfortable level of illumination, while the researchers gradually reduced the level of the lighting for the test group. The efficiency of both groups steadily rose—until the light-starved group complained that they couldn't see what they were doing and had to stop.

Then the researchers turned devious. According to the Western Electric report:

> This time they asked the girls [again, coil winders] how they felt about the changes in illumination. When they increased the light, the girls said they liked it, could work better under the bright light. Then they *pretended* to increase the light, and the girls said they liked it even better. When they decreased the light, and then told the girls, the latter commented unfavorably. They then only *pretended* to decrease the light, and the girls said the dimmer light was not so pleasant to work under. Throughout this experiment, production did not materially change.

Exactly what was going on with those groups of Hawthorne coil winders toiling away in their shifting levels of light has been the subject of debate among engineers, psychologists, and managers to the present day.

These initial illumination studies blossomed into additional experiments and attracted participation by two researchers from Harvard, George Elton Mayo and Frist Roethlisberger. In 1927, they moved the action into the relay assembly room. Five women were selected to do the repetitive work of "putting together a coil, armature, contact springs and insulators in a fixture and securing the parts in position by means of four machine screws," a hand assembly operation that took about a minute. The women worked together for a period of two and a half years. During that time, the researchers tinkered with many variables, including:

- The size of the room in which the women worked.
- The lighting, ventilation, room layout, and equipment.
- The number of different types of relays assembled.

- When, how much, and by what standard the women were paid.
- When, how often, and for how long they took rest breaks. No breaks, fewer and longer breaks, more frequent and shorter breaks, were all tried.
- The relationship between the women and their supervisors and their observers.
- When, what, and how much the women ate at lunchtime.
- Whether the company restaurant provided lunch (sandwich, beverage, and fruit or pudding) or the women brought their own.
- The length of the work day and the work week. (The standard schedule was a twelve-hour day and a five-and-a-half-day week.)
- The relationships among the women.
- The size of the working group.
- Whether the women could or could not talk among themselves, while they worked.
- Non-work-related personal issues (home life, romantic relationships).
- General health, diet, sleep habits.
- Amount of supervision.

Although output of this small team of assemblers fluctuated in response to the many and various changes in conditions, overall it increased during the two-and-a-half-year period. In addition, the morale of the women picked up and their relationship to the researchers improved. According to the account of Roethlisberger and Dickson, "their first line supervisor ceased to be one who 'bawled them out' in case things went wrong; instead he came to be regarded as a friendly representative of management."

More experiments were conducted, in other areas of the plant, and an interviewing program began that eventually included about 22,000 employees—more than half the population of that massive factory. Although Juran was not directly involved in the experiments, he worked within this atmosphere of testing, exploration, and analysis of the effects of the cultural and human aspects of work.

At Hawthorne, and other factories, the Taylor Method generally served to reduce the importance and contribution of the individual line worker. But the Hawthorne Illumination Studies demonstrated that some factory managers and academic researchers sensed that Taylorism—even in its earliest days—had significant effects on human behavior. Yet the researchers did not seem to connect the issues of behavior directly to the structure of the organization. Mayo wrote: "We may take it as decided that it is far too easily possible for an intelligent worker to experience something of futility and exasperation in modern industry and business, although little can as yet be said of its occasion." In other words, the mystery seemed to lie within the worker, rather than within the system. This impulse to blame—or credit—the individual person, rather than the system within which he or she works, although completely antithetical to quality management principles, persists to this day.

❀

CLIMBING THE LADDER

Juran settled comfortably in to his life at Hawthorne. The family moved from downtown Chicago to a nicer apartment in Cicero, near the plant. Joe joined the Hawthorne Chess Club and swiftly established himself as champion, as he had at the University of Minnesota, often engaging in matches with other AT&T facilities via telephone, games that could take twelve hours to complete. In one game against the corporate rivals in New York, Juran defeated Don Quarles to give Hawthorne its first-ever victory over the Easterners. The Hawthorne Club even played against the Antwerp office of Western Electric, making the moves by mail, in a game that lasted for years. Juran also tried his skills against world-class competitors. He played Emanuel Lasker, a former world chess champion who is still considered one of the greatest players of all time, to a draw.

And Juran continued his rise up the corporate ladder. In 1929, at age 24, he was promoted to supervisor of all engineers in the Inspection Branch and he began to demonstrate his shortcomings as a manager. He had little tolerance for peers who blocked his way or couldn't keep up with him. "I tended to be impatient with those who could not keep up with my own pace. I was awkward and even puerile in dealing with many personnel problems." Most of his assignments at Hawthorne involved investigating mistakes and problems and determining what or who had caused them. Once he had analyzed a situation, he would write a report to his managers, often in blunt and unforgiving language. Although his colleagues accepted that his observations were usually accurate, they often chafed at the way he expressed them. He searched for blame, rather than seeking to work collaboratively to solve a problem. Although this approach was partly the result of the system within which he worked, it also seems to have been part of his nature.

The tension with his colleagues only grew worse when he became responsible for evaluating their jobs and setting their wages. "I could outthink and outdo most of them, and I nevertheless expected them to keep up with me. When they could not, which was often, I could be sharply critical and even cruel." But his limitations as a manager of people did not, at first, deter his rise. At the time, the reward for performance and the measure of corporate success was one's position on the hierarchical ladder. "If somebody did well, they'd make him boss and if he did well at that, they'd make him a bigger boss, and so on. It wasn't that clearly seen that leadership was very different from technological analysis and the like," says Juran. In other words, management was not yet well understood as a profession, nor were there ways to reward superior performers in any other way than pushing them up the ladder—sometimes to the point where they became ineffectual. In 1969, Dr. Laurence J. Peter wrote *The Peter Principle: Why Things*

Always Go Wrong, a satirical commentary on his experiences with educational and other organizations. "In a hierarchy," wrote Peter, "every employee tends to rise to his level of incompetence."

Juran now sees his attitude as stemming from his difficult childhood, particularly his experiences with anti-Semitism. "When I got to be a manager, starting to have power, I began to get my vengeance. I started getting even with the world. When I look back at it, it's stupid. The people I was getting revenge on had nothing to do with what happened when I was a youngster. It was completely irrational, but I did it anyway. You know, the human brain is wired in mysterious ways."

DEPRESSION AND DOWNSIZING

The profusion of study and activity at Hawthorne—the application of statistical methods and the inquiry into human relations—came crashing to a halt with the Depression. The Hawthorne Works suffered reductions in business and in the workforce that make some of the downsizing of the late 1980s and 1990s look relatively small. Sales at Western Electric plummeted from $411 million in 1929 to less than $79 million in 1933—an 80 percent drop. Employment at Hawthorne crashed right along with the numbers at the top line: 43,000 people had worked at the "worker's paradise" of Hawthorne in 1929. By 1933 the number hit 6,000—a reduction of 37,000 workers, or about 86 percent. At first, Western Electric management sought to find alternate work for its employees. The company created Make Work programs and busied their idle machines with the manufacture of jigsaw puzzles and cigarette lighters. But the carnage could not be avoided.

"All of a sudden the world started to collapse around me," remembers Juran. People who had served the company for decades, and thought themselves secure, found themselves suddenly without a job and with no means of supporting their families or paying their mortgages. "I saw this as a very real threat to myself. By that time, I had three little kiddies, and my biggest concern was, 'Are they going to have to endure the poverty that I went through?' I was really terrified about the prospect."

Juran, at 28, one of the youngest managers in the plant, survived the cuts. But, still worried about his prospects, he sought to add another arrow to his professional quiver. He decided to earn a law degree, and enrolled at Loyola University in Chicago in 1931, studying afternoons and nights. "I could do that, because we were working short hours. My standard of living actually went up during the Big Depression because prices went down so much. I was getting, by that time, a good salary, so I could afford to go to school." He received his JD in January 1935 and was admitted to the Illinois Bar in 1936, although he never became a practicing attorney. Continuing his move up the corporate ladder, he was promoted to broader supervisory duties in 1931 and again in 1934, as the national economy began to brighten.

The study of law forced Juran to think differently than he had as an engineer. "You have to think about the meaning of the language, and separate out the nuances. And the reverse of that, of course, is the ability to communicate with precision. To write and speak in ways that permit no misunderstanding." Juran's writing, when he began to publish in the mid-1940s, exhibited clarity and directness. "Your writing is so simple!" said Peter Drucker.

MANAGERIAL ENDGAME

In the fall of 1937, Juran's boss, A. B. Hazard, invited him to come to corporate headquarters in New York City and become Head of the Industrial Engineering Department. In his new job, Juran was responsible for job evaluations, time studies, and wage and salary determination for all Western Electric factories, of which there were now three.

The family moved to Summit, New Jersey, "a perfectly delight-ful bedroom community of the Metropolitan area. It had good schools, good community services and still other essentials of a good place to live. It also harbored religious and racial prejudices which would rise to plague us." Juran liked Summit, however, and became active in community activities, including the schools and Cub Scouts.

Juran learned a great deal during his four years in New York. He participated in the New York-based management societies, including the Society for the Advancement of Management (SAM) and the American Management Association (AMA). He developed a network of colleagues in management, took speaking engagements, and wrote articles.

To help him determine competitive compensation levels, he would sometimes visit other large companies to conduct a form of bench-marking regarding wages and salaries. On one visit to General Motors, his prowess at problem solving and cryptanalysis enabled him to pick up an idea that he would use later in formulating the Pareto Principle.

At that time, General Motors used an IBM computer system based on punch cards. The wages of each employee were recorded on a card, and whenever a change in wages was proposed—often by a union—the staff would run the cards through the computer to determine the effect on payroll. For one test, the staff members miswired the plug-board of the card readers so that, when the cards emerged, instead of printing English and usable figures, they printed gibberish. The IBM staff members got excited, seeing this as a way to use the wiring of a plugboard to create an unbreakable code.

But to Juran, who had deciphered Rashi as a boy and specialized in cryptanalysis in the Signal Corps Reserve, "It didn't seem that big a deal. So, I ended up taking several of these things to my hotel and had to stay up with it until about three in the morning, but I broke the code. Next morning, when I came back to them, they were stunned. They had talked themselves into believing this thing is in-soluble and here this guy solved it." As a result, one of the staff mem-bers let this visiting miracle worker in on a confidential study he had made of the distribution of salaries at General Motors. It was, he said, based on the work of Vilfredo Pareto, an Italian economist. "We discussed it," says Juran. "I checked his mathematics. I didn't see that we could use that at Western Electric. But the name Pareto I latched on to, put it into my memory in case I ever needed it." Not many years later, he did.

But the transition from factory manager to corporate executive proved difficult. Juran found himself without the skills necessary to play the corporate game of politics, maneuvering, alliance making, and self-promoting—a game every bit as elaborate as chess. "My record of being able to outthink the others as to my specialty deluded me into assuming I could also outthink others as to their specialty, and these others included not only my peers but also their superiors and even my own superiors. All this arrogance received due discussion among men who were in a position to influence my progress. None of them may have been a match for me individually, but collectively I was no match for them, not even close. So there built up, gradually, the forces needed to put me in my place."

Life became increasingly uncomfortable for Juran at corporate headquarters at 195 Broadway in Manhattan. The man who had invited Juran to New York left the company. He was replaced by a manager whom Juran had offended in the past. Juran, miffed that he hadn't been promoted into the position, resented his new boss. Soon, Juran was being excluded from important meetings. The hated boss was promoted to a higher position and, again, Juran was not promoted into his place.

But not all Juran's past associates felt negatively toward him. Charles Terrel had recommended Juran to the administrator of a new government agency, known informally as "Lend-Lease." When the Japanese attacked the U.S. base at Pearl Harbor on December 7, 1941, the role of Lend-Lease took on wartime urgency. Within a few days, Juran received a telegram from Edward R. Stettinius Jr., the head of Lend-Lease, asking Juran to come to Washington for six weeks to help set up a statistical department.

Juran leaped at the chance to help out with the war effort. Just as the horrid tales of pogroms and the taunts of anti-Semitic neighbors had haunted Juran as a boy in Romania and Minnesota, he vividly felt the threat of Nazism as the war spread in Europe. Perhaps equally important, the Lend-Lease job provided Juran with an escape route from the gathering political battle at Western Electric. He secured a leave of absence and—always the workaholic—reported for work on Christmas Day, 1941.

3

The $42-Billion Garden Hose

(1941–1945)

Never before have we had so little time
in which to do so much.

Franklin D. Roosevelt

A SEETHING HATRED

Juran plunged into his Lend-Lease assignment with a patriotic zeal intensified by mounting anxiety over his professional position and infused with what he calls a "seething hatred" of the Nazis. The hatred was made all the more vivid and immediate by his perception that anti-Semitism had contributed to his career difficulties at Western Electric corporate headquarters.

He rented a room in Washington, intending to stay there for the six weeks of the planned leave, and to visit his family in Summit, New Jersey on the weekends. The absence would mean hardship for the Jurans. A fourth child, Donald, had been born in March. Mrs. Juran did not drive a car. The three older children had not completely overcome the sense of disruption caused by the move to New York from Chicago four years earlier. The oldest son, Robert, was having behavioral problems that required the Jurans to seek extensive, and expensive, medical and psychiatric advice.

Arriving in Washington, Juran looked the role of an entrenched, even bemired, mid-level corporate manager: gray at the temples, thick around the neck and chin. But at Lend-Lease he found himself in a very different type of bureaucracy than the one that had stymied him at Western Electric. The staff of the Office of Lend-Lease Administration (OLLA) resembled a "pick-up team," as he later called it—an intriguing mix of long-time government employees and a variety of outsiders from academia, industry, and law. Edward Stettinius, Jr., the Lend-Lease Administrator—the general manager—had been a successful executive at General Motors, and then Chairman of U.S. Steel. Later, in 1943, he would be named Roosevelt's Secretary of State. George Ball, who went on to become Undersecretary of State for Presidents Kennedy and Johnson, was General Counsel to one of the OLLA departments in which Juran served. Juran found these colleagues more worldly than the executives at Western Electric. Many of them had a broader education than Juran, and they were deeply concerned with issues that were more complex than those involving labor relations and compensation levels, which Juran had dealt with as a corporate middle-manager. They were thinking about human relations on a global scale.

The practical challenges of the Lend-Lease Administration were well-suited to Juran's skills in analysis and problem solving. His six-week assignment was to help OLLA set up a statistical department. In fact, the department had already been established, and the six-week stint was more in the nature of a tryout for Juran. At the end of the assignment, Stettinius asked him to stay on as Assistant Administrator. The Signal Corps also invited Juran to join its ranks, to help out with their ongoing problems of quality control. Juran chose OLLA and signed on at a salary equivalent to the amount he had been earning at Western Electric: $9,000. "I had every reason to spend the rest of the war in government service. I was genuinely dedicated to winning that war, especially as to the Nazis, whom I loathed with a fury. I concluded I could do best in the Lend-Lease organization on the theory that they needed managers, which were in short supply. Again, I was assuming that I had managerial skills, and I was mistaken."

Lend-Lease faced a challenge as urgent and intense as the building of a nationwide telephone network had been at Western Electric, but of much greater significance—it seemed to be about saving the world. The challenge required the cooperation of not just one complex and bureaucratic organization, but many, and involved a heady mix of politics, academics, and history, all with an undercurrent of fear. The idea of Lend-Lease had come from President Roosevelt, intended as a way to support Great Britain in its fight against Germany, while still keeping the United States officially in compliance with the Neutrality Acts, which had been established starting in 1935. A stipulation of these Acts was that U.S. suppliers could only provide goods to the Allies on a cash basis. By late 1940, Britain was in desperate need of war matériel, but painfully short of cash as a result of the losses suffered and money consumed in defending England.

In June 1940, France had signed an armistice with Germany, which left Great Britain as the only Allied power in Western Europe still opposing Germany and the occupied countries of the Axis. In July, Britain refused Hitler's overtures of peace and, by August, Britain felt the nearly crushing force of Germany's power: prolonged bombing attacks on British ports and radar stations, then aircraft factories and Royal Air Force (RAF) installations, and finally cities, including London. The attacks were intended to weaken British morale, damage military defenses, and reduce fighting reserves, and so prepare the way for a German invasion. But the British responded heroically, pitting RAF Spitfire fighter aircraft against the great waves of German bombers droning in from bases on the Continent. After 57 days of what became known as the Battle of Britain, Germany deferred its plans for invasion—the first major setback for the Germans in World War II.

President Franklin Roosevelt was determined to help Britain, but he needed an innovative, politically feasible solution—one that avoided the use of cash. His idea was to lend or lease war materials to those countries "whose defense was vital to the defense of the United States." In a press conference held on December 17, 1940, he described the intention of the Lend-Lease Act with a homely analogy. "Suppose my neighbor's house catches fire," he said, "and I have a length of garden hose four or five hundred feet away. If I can take my garden hose and connect it up with his hydrant, I may help him to put out that fire. Now what do I do? I don't say to him before that operation, 'Neighbor, my garden hose cost me $15; you have to pay me for it.' What is this transaction that goes on? I don't want $15—I want my garden hose back after the fire is over."

The idea provoked tremendous controversy. Isolationists viewed Lend-Lease as a dangerous first step that would propel us inexorably into the war. Those in favor of the idea argued that, in fact, it would help keep the United States out of the war and save American lives. Lend-Lease was hotly debated, but finally passed by Congress on March 11, 1941, authorizing Roosevelt to "sell, transfer, exchange, lend, lease, or otherwise dispose of any defense article the president deems vital to the defense of the United States." That opened the door for the United States to send what would eventually total $42 billion worth of civilian and military items—raw materials, manufactured products, food, and machinery—to 47 Allied countries from March 1941 to August 1945, when President Harry S. Truman ordered the end of Lend-Lease.

Even after it was passed, Lend-Lease remained controversial. Many Americans worried that we would not be paid back. Others felt it would disrupt world trade. Many were disturbed that Lend-Lease provided for aid to the Soviet Union as well as to countries not directly involved in the war. And the public, when asked to cope with shortages of food and other consumer products at home, often grumbled and blamed Lend-Lease.

But, to Juran, being part of Lend-Lease meant "striking a blow at the Nazis. It was a way to serve the country."

THE BEDROOM BOTTLENECK

As an organization, the Lend-Lease Administration faced two major "business" challenges. First, the demand for its goods—starting with aircraft, tanks and guns, and ammunition, and, within a year, food and other nonmilitary supplies—far exceeded the available supply. Second, the goods were needed urgently, desperately, *now*—not tomorrow or next year. In mid-1941, Germany was widening the war, advancing on Greece and Yugoslavia and the countries of North Africa. Delivery of needed goods to the Allied forces was a matter of customer *survival,* rather than customer satisfaction.

Roosevelt had no interest in setting up a large government agency to administer the Lend-Lease program. The departments of War, Navy, Treasury, and Agriculture already had the infrastructure to handle the tasks of procurement and delivery; Lend-Lease would only serve as an agency for administration and coordination. Roosevelt originally assigned responsibility for managing Lend-Lease to Harry Hopkins, his long-time colleague and adviser. Hopkins had a great deal of government experience, as head of the Works Progress Administration (WPA) and subsequently as Secretary of Commerce, but did not have much managerial expertise. According to Doris Kearns Goodwin, seventeen rooms in the Federal Reserve Building were made available to Hopkins and his thirty-five member staff, but Hopkins preferred to work from his bedroom on the second floor of the White House.

Within three hours of signing the Lend-Lease Act, President Roosevelt issued two directives. The first called for the delivery of torpedo boats, depth charges, guns, and ammunition to the British. The second called for supplying Greece—then under threat from the Germans—with guns and howitzers and shells. In April, Yugoslavia—also under attack by Germany—made a request for a great deal of equipment, including 100 bombers, 100 fighter planes, 100 tanks, 2,000 trucks, a large number of guns, and much more. The demand could not be satisfied. "We had too little to send, and we could not get it there fast enough," wrote Stettinius. Both Greece and Yugoslavia fell to the Nazis.

The next emergency was in North Africa. If Hitler could take Egypt, the Suez Canal might be lost, and with it, the entire Middle East. Egypt needed planes and trucks and, most urgently, light tanks for use in the desert. In March 1941, the entire U.S. production of tanks was just 16. In that spring, Britain ran short of food. Lend-Lease promptly sent 100,000 cases of evaporated milk, 11,000 tons of cheese, and 11,000 tons of eggs. The Department of Agriculture went into the open market and bought large quantities of canned and frozen meats and fish, frozen and powdered eggs, dried and canned vegetables, and evaporated and powdered milk—and kept the shipments up through the end of the year.

From the beginning, it was clear that, in order to meet the huge demand for war supplies, American production capacity had to be increased and the speed of development and manufacture had to accelerate as well. By December 7, 1941, when Pearl Harbor was attacked, some $5.5 billion in war contracts had been awarded to American manufacturers. In addition, hundreds of millions were invested in building or improving factories, shipyards, processing plants, and storage and distribution facilities. Auto makers (Ford, Chrysler, Packard, General Motors, Kaiser) and aircraft manufacturers (Douglas, Boeing, Bell, Grumman), shipbuilders and others, joined in the effort. It was a massive conversion of American industry, changing from "automobile wheels to gun mounts, from fireworks to ammunition, and from cotton mill machinery to howitzers for mountain fighting."

But the tremendous demand for material and the requests flooding in from all around the world were far too great a burden for the bedroom administration of Harry Hopkins. "By the end of the summer of 1941, Lend-Lease was rapidly evolving into a broad program of production and delivery of rapidly growing extent and complexity. As it did so, the administrative burden grew correspondingly heavier. Besides all the problems of production, there was the pressing problem of delivering the goods by sea and by air."

Hopkins worked at a card table in his bedroom, with—as Goodwin describes it—the "documents and papers spilling off chairs and tables." Things were getting further and further behind. In August 1941, the economist John Maynard Keynes—serving in Roosevelt's government—spoke of the costly delays: "If we are to be honest with ourselves, we must admit that the switch over from cash purchase to Lend-Lease has retarded the war effort by six months." By the fall of 1941, the average time required to process a requisition was more than ninety days. More than 1,200 uncleared requisitions were strewn around Hopkins' bedroom.

Roosevelt concluded that more had to be done to mobilize American industry, so that companies could produce more goods faster than ever before. And, he realized, the Lend-Lease Administration had become a bottleneck in the specification, procurement, and shipping of these goods. He decided to call on experienced managers from the private sector to set up a simple and flexible administration to manage the allocation and distribution of America's vast resources.

PROFESSIONAL MANAGEMENT

"I received a message one morning from Harry Hopkins," wrote Stettinius, "asking if I could come over to the White House to see him. Hopkins was not well at the time and I was shown into his bedroom. He was sitting up, working over a pile of papers on a bed-table in front of him. The first thing he said was, 'Ed, the President wants you to take over administration of the Lend-Lease program. The President thinks there's nothing more important now for the country than getting this Lend-Lease show moving at top speed.'"

Stettinius accepted the job, took over the post in August and, by the end of October, had established the Office of Lend-Lease Administration. He was given authority to exercise all the powers conferred by the Lend-Lease Act with two exceptions: (1) the designation of Lend-Lease countries and (2) negotiation of the Lend-Lease master agreements. He was authorized to transfer supplies within the first Congressional allocation of $7 billion.

Even with its new status and substantial spending authority, OLLA faced an onerous organizational challenge in getting its work done. But the original idea remained the same: to keep OLLA small and sharply focused on administration, with the actual work of procurement and distribution handled through existing departments. OLLA would receive all requests for material, determine whether they should be filled, route the request to the appropriate department (food to Agriculture, ships to the Navy, and so on), expedite shipping, and keep careful accounts of all transactions. In doing so, OLLA would have to manage a highly complex process that required the cooperation of many departments, each with its own well-established culture, processes, and systems. Stettinius's task was to streamline (current term: redesign) the process, so the amount of time it took to fulfill a request could be drastically reduced.

The cumbersome, inefficient nature of this setup showed most clearly in the paperwork. At the beginning of his tenure with Lend-Lease, Stettinius saw that the confusion and duplication were "perfectly unbelievable." He hired Thomas McCabe, president of the Scott Paper Company, to conduct a thorough survey of the Lend-Lease process and find ways to reduce duplication, weed out overlapping functions, and make the requisition process more flexible. One of Juran's first assignments, as one of a dozen assistant administrators, was to "make provision for supplies, facilities and services."

The assignment placed Juran in his favorite role—as a roving, project-based problem solver—and he "went into that absolutely to the hilt. I was working 80, 90, 100 hours a week." Juran assembled a team, with members from about a dozen government agencies, including the Treasury Department, the Customs Bureau, as well as from the foreign government missions, including those from Great Britain and the Soviet Union, among others. It quickly became clear that, although each of the agencies knew its own job, none of them understood the overall process of getting products from a factory, onto a boat, and to their final customers. Juran saw that, in order to expedite shipments, he would have to arm his committee members with the necessary knowledge of the whole process. "In its earlier deliberations," Juran wrote in the final report, "the committee attempted to make minor improvements here and there in the procedures, but found that the pattern was too closely interwoven to permit such action. Accordingly, the committee abandoned such efforts and undertook to develop a new system specially designed for war purposes."

The team gathered up the documents involved in the process—eighteen in all—tabulated all the bits of information, and laid them out in a graphic display, like a spreadsheet, so that the team members could see the whole process. They realized that many of the documents duplicated information that had been submitted on the other documents, and was being modified or copied simply to fit a particular department's own format. In 1941, before the arrival of photocopiers, copying required rewriting or retyping. Thus, every transfer of information from one document to another offered an opportunity for error, and a minor error in typing could lead to a major blunder in fulfillment. The wrong material might be placed in the wrong box or be delivered to the wrong destination. A soldier who needed bullets might receive a can of tuna instead.

Working together, Juran's team reduced the total number of documents required in the process by 50 percent. They redesigned other documents so that key information was displayed in a way that made copying easier. The result: less typing and retyping, greater accuracy, less delay, and a reduction in the time required to prepare documents.

The reduction in paperwork contributed to a reduction in the time it took to process a request. By February of 1942, Stettinius calculated that Juran and his team had reduced Hopkins's 90-day fulfillment time to about 53 hours. Juran looks back on the effort as "a very useful accomplishment. In a way, I was surprised. I was no expert in government operations but, nevertheless, here was a problem that lent itself to analysis by tools that I was familiar with and which could be applied anywhere. It stands out as one of the big quality improvement projects of all time."

But not everyone in the agency viewed the streamlining as an improvement. A letter of evaluation of Juran by his supervisor, in October 1942, expressed worry that some staff members who depended on certain types of information had not been consulted about the changes and that some had lost information they needed or forms they had relied on. The supervisor begins the letter by saying that some of Juran's initiatives had "started off on the wrong foot," and continues: "I called Mr. Juran's attention to these conditions, and told him that I felt that some arrangements should be made whereby there would be closer contacts between the operating division and the Records and Reports Division, and I was told that I should get around more and find out what was going on."

Anyone who has worked to change an entrenched process in a bureaucracy knows that it generally ruffles a few feathers, at the very
least. But Juran seems to have exacerbated the naturally disruptive
nature of his work with the same abrasive approach that had rankled
colleagues at Western Electric. The supervisor characterizes Juran's
attitude, as it related to reports and records, as "destructive rather than
constructive." A Lend-Lease organization chart, dated September
1943, shows Juran in a lonely rectangle far to one side, under the
telling title *Special Assignments,* with no direct reports and no immediate supervisor.

But, despite these signs of managerial inadequacy, Juran stayed on
and on at Lend-Lease. Late in the summer of 1942, after six months
as a weekend husband and father, Juran moved his family from Summit, New Jersey, to the Washington suburb of Arlington, Virginia.
The move seemed to place a greater burden on the family than had the
separation. Juran, as usual, gave his work top priority. Robert, the eldest son, now began to skip school and engage in minor vandalism
and petty theft. "All this took place during the strain of living in the
Washington area in wartime, with all the shortages and the problems
of transport, of shopping, and even of standard of living. Our standard
was going down due to the inflation in prices while the government
salaries failed to keep pace." Despite his difficulties with the Lend-
Lease culture, the work continued to be a success. Each year, Juran
asked Western Electric for an extension of his leave of absence, and
each year—1942, 1943, 1944—it was granted.

In 1943, Juran helped prepare the report to Congress, requesting
an extension of the Lend-Lease budget, which was approved. Lend-
Lease came to be known as one of the most effective organizations in
the capital, with a relatively small staff, which never exceeded 600
people. "[The] Office of Lend-Lease Administration was unique in
war-time Washington, a compact, efficiently managed, economy-
minded oasis in a desert of empire-builders, proliferating payrolls, inefficiency and reckless spending." Even the press admired Lend-Lease.
The *Washington Post* reported that "Mr. Stettinius has done as much

The $42-Billion Garden Hose   6 5

and perhaps more than any man in Washington to show how to set up a war agency and how to conduct it without bureaucratic feuds and without obscurity and confusion."

Many years later, a magazine interviewer asked Juran what he considered to be the most extraordinary thing that happened in his lifetime, and he replied, "The time I spent in World War II in the federal government as an assistant administrator in the Lend-Lease program. It opened my eyes to some very big forces in the economy, world affairs, and politics." Not only did he find himself playing on a much broader and more exciting playing field, he also gained further insights into the subject of management. Stettinius, in particular, offered an intriguing model of a highly successful executive. Stettinius had a "commitment to the new industrial order emerging in the 1930s. He brought an open mind to corporate problems. He intuitively sensed the importance of changing relationships between business, labor, and government. Infused with a deep strain of social consciousness, he sought to make industry more responsible to the public upon which it ultimately depended."

Juran talked of Stettinius in a very different way than he had of his managers at Western Electric. "Stet is fun to work for," he wrote. "Stet has contagious enthusiasm. Stet has a sense of planning how to accomplish. Stet is a natural manager."

DECISION TIME

Juran's stint at Lend-Lease provided more than a sabbatical from his career at Western Electric; it gave him an opportunity to see himself more clearly and to think analytically about what he had learned in his years in industry. The example of Stettinius and the continuing difficulties of working in a bureaucracy, as well as the unpleasant prospect of returning to the complications of life at Western Electric headquarters, brought him to the conclusion that he was not a "natural manager" and did not belong in a big organization. He watched, as many of his colleagues at Lend-Lease began to climb the ladder of the government hierarchy. Stettinius left OLLA in 1943 to become Undersecretary of State and then Secretary. Juran wrote that the war agencies had created "unheard-of opportunities for the bolder elements of the citizenry. Within a space of months some were holding down jobs which had been lifetime goals." But he saw no future for himself in the government. "While a number of the people that were in the Lend-Lease organization ended up in pretty high government posts, I wasn't one of them. And I don't think it was possible for me to do that because of my lack of experience." Even so, Juran had proved that his skills were transferable from industry to government. He had made a contribution and been recognized for it. And he began to realize that many of the problems and challenges he had helped solve in the Lend-Lease organization were similar to those he had solved at Western Electric—and probably were endemic to all large organizations.

These conclusions motivated Juran to write. At the end of 1943, his workload eased—Lend-Lease was functioning smoothly, and the decisive action now was occurring on the battlefield—and he began to thoughtfully consider his next career move. "For the first time, I began to think, 'What am I going to do when this is over?'" He had long had the urge to write seriously, and had published his first article in 1935, although such activity was frowned on at Western Electric. "The atmosphere was actually forbidding," Juran remembers. "Many of the important managers in that factory were people who had come up from the ranks. The deal was, if you're taking time to write papers, you're probably neglecting your job." This attitude contrasted sharply with that of Bell Labs, which was populated by scientists for whom publishing was a central and valued pursuit, just as it is in academia.

In 1943, with some free time available among the long hours at OLLA, Juran turned his mind to a book. The subject: the problems of management in the federal government. Juran sold the book to Harper

& Brothers, with the help of a friend and vice president there, Ordway Tead, whom he had met through the Society for the Advancement of Managers (SAM). *Bureaucracy, A Challenge to Better Management—A Constructive Analysis of Management Effectiveness in the Federal Government* appeared in the spring of 1944. The book does not specifically examine Lend-Lease (although it is dedicated to his colleagues there); rather, it generalizes about Juran's experiences in government. "The student of management is amazed as well as shocked to see the state of management hygiene prevailing in the bureaucratic world," he writes in *Bureaucracy*. "Many tools of modern management are just waiting to be used."

Juran employs an allegorical style (likening the development of government to the creation, and the limiting of staff to birth control) to explore, in a work of 136 pages, how government is organized, the problems that plague its operations, and, in conclusion, a program for "better management in government." The program contains nine suggested improvements; for example, each government agency should create a "legally authoritative statement of objectives"; "standards of performance should be established for all operations"; "the functions of the Federal government should be performed using a minimum of personnel, time, equipment, and materials"; and "the management function would be recognized as essential to the carrying out of the duties of the Federal government." The book, in short, argues that the principles of business management—still nascent, even in industry—should be applied to the sprawling chaos of government. It is an idea that still has currency.

The book received positive reviews. "J. M. Juran's *Bureaucracy* is refreshing and creative," judged Willard Shelton in *Book Week*, "and, I suspect, may be immediately useful." J. M. Gaus reviewed the book for the *Yale Law Review* and found Juran's approach to be "in such refreshing contrast to most writing on this topic that we can well be content with what we have here and ask for a sequel." The book eventually sold out its modest run of 1,500 copies, but was not reprinted in paperback. Juran was delighted to have a book published and hoped it would do some good. The book also increased Juran's status as a public figure and an expert in management, and he found himself sought after for speaking engagements and quoted in the press. A *Fortune* article called *Doctors of Management* quotes him: "J. M. Juran, an engineer now in a war-agency job, estimates that the 'government population' could be cut in half and still perform all its functions with at least its present effectiveness." Encouraged by the reaction to his first book, Juran began work on a second volume and started thinking about a third.

In late 1944 or early 1945—while Juran was still mulling over his career decision—he had a pivotal conversation with his boss at Western Electric, a new vice-president, Stan Bracken. Bracken had considered Juran's case and concluded that he should not have made the move from Hawthorne to Western Electric headquarters and, in fact, that Juran was not qualified to hold any job as a senior manager. "He told me this bluntly, and he was dead right. There was no threat about it, as he also concluded that there was no non-managerial job I could not do. So it became clear that there was now a ceiling to my progress in the managerial sense. I could remain, have a comfortable post and salary at some middle level and complete a career that way. I brooded plenty at this turn of events. The idea of an end to 'progress' was revolting, since I did not at that time realize the 'progress' need not involve being a manager. Neither was I objective about my own contributions to my defeat. Instead, I looked for enemies under the beds. Spies, anti-Semites, tale-bearers and the rest."

No doubt, anti-Semitism existed at the Western Electric headquarters, as it did within many corporations of the day. Even at the Hawthorne Works, Juran could identify only three Jews among the hundreds of managers employed there. Later, as a consultant, he would experience far more overt anti-Semitism. But, like his father, Juran did not actively involve himself in Jewish societies or activities, and many of his associates—even those who considered themselves to be his friends—were unaware that he was Jewish. During the course of his brooding, Juran concluded that, although anti-Semitism probably did play a role in his difficulties, "the main problem was my own conduct."

Juran began to consider alternatives to the big ship that had rescued him from the sea of poverty and the wretchedness of his youth. He knew that, although he certainly had proved his shortcomings as a manager—at both Western Electric and Lend-Lease—he had also unquestionably proved his skills as an analyst and problem solver. He considered going freelance: "I was 40 years old, and still merchantable and had begun to get some degree of public recognition, had a decent track record, hadn't moved around, stayed with one company, and so on. It was a risk I was willing to take. I knew that it was a risk for the family. But I also knew that if I went back to The Bell System I'd be able to inch up further and so on. But I wouldn't have been happy, and that would have had its effect on the family, anyway. For me it would have been just an endless inner turmoil."

In August 1944, he wrote to his younger sister, Charlotte: "You are by now probably aware that my stay in the Government has left its permanent scars. It is unlikely that I will go back to Industry, and even more unlikely that I will return to the green pastures of the Western Electric Company. But what I will not do is much more clear than what I will do. It is likely that I am heading back to whence I started— to whatever fields will leave me free to let imagination run riot, to read, to write and to speak whatever pleases me, and to achieve eminence in search of the great truths. None of this is flowery—it is what I shall do (unless someone is in the way). When that time comes you will find me well traveled and quite exciting company, as will also be the case with Sadie. There is much fun ahead. It is going to be a good world again. It will have many of the mechanical things we Americans love, and the rest of the world will learn to love them also. But much more than this, we are entering an intensely fascinating era of development of human thinking—how nations can get along with each other, and how they may keep the peace for a long long time. Even if you are on the sidelines it will be a fascinating thing to watch. But I intend to be on the playing field."

For all his uncertainty, Juran clearly felt optimistic, even exhila-
rated, about the prospects for himself and the postwar world. And so
he made his decision. "I decided that here's this field of management
which I definitely know a good deal about. My conclusion was, I'm
going to spend the rest of my life on that subject and I'm going to be
the complete renaissance man with respect to it. I'm going to philos-
ophize, theorize; I'll lecture, I'll write, I'll consult, I'll do the works.
But there was no ready-made job. I had to piece it together."

4

Launching the Canoe of Consultancy

(1945–1954)

*. . . to launch our frail canoe on the
ocean of enterprise . . .*

Wilkins Micawber,
in *David Copperfield*

※

PIECING IT TOGETHER

D uring 1944, Juran wrote a second book, *Management of In-spection and Quality Control.* It appeared in the spring of 1945, and provided a thorough discussion of the issues involved in how to manage the quality function and its role in the organization. The book was reviewed, in manuscript form, by the major figures in quality at the time—including Shewhart, Deming, Harold Dodge, and Colonel Leslie E. Simon, whose 1932 book, *An Engineers' Man-ual of Statistical Methods,* was considered the quality control "bible" at the time. Like Juran's first book, *Management of Inspection* received good notices and gained attention from the quality journals and the general press. The *New York Times* reviewer, Lee Cooper, captured the essence of Juran's approach: "He sets forth the general technique of scientific management and more efficient operation, but leaves the adaptation of these principles in any given case to the plant operators and owners." *Industrial Quality Control* bestowed on it that perennial epithet, "must reading."

On the title page of the 1945 book, the author is identified as "Formerly Chief of Inspection Control Division, Western Electric." So, although he had yet to officially resign, his decision to leave ob-viously had been made. In doing so, Juran would be taking a finan-cial risk. He had logged twenty-one years of service at Western Electric (including the four years at Lend-Lease) but he needed twenty-five years to receive the money in his pension. He abandoned it. When they learned of this, Juran's colleagues were stunned; they could not believe that he would toss away twenty-one years of accu-mulated pension and a job virtually guaranteed for life. It was Juran's great risk, similar in audacity to his father's move to America, and his grandfather's flight over the Carpathian mountains.

Juran knew that publishing alone could not provide his family with sufficient income. *Management of Inspection* retailed for $3. Even

73

if the entire printing of 5,000 sold out (which it eventually did), after the publisher's discount to the retailer, Juran could not expect to receive more than a couple of thousand dollars in royalties. And, given the standard payment practices of publishers, the money would trickle in over a period of two or three years. So, book writing could not be counted on to come close to the comfortable $9,000 salary Juran had grown accustomed to at Western Electric and then at Lend-Lease. He needed a base of operations and a guaranteed income, at least for the tenuous early years of his new career.

While at Western Electric headquarters in New York, one of Juran's duties was to develop and maintain contacts with members of academia. He had had contact with two professors at New York University, Leon P. Alford, who was active and well-known in the field of business management, and David Porter, an expert in motion and time studies. Alford was keen to have Juran join the NYU faculty, and the two arranged for Juran to meet with the Dean of NYU's Engineering College, Thorndike Saville. Juran struck a deal with Saville: He would become head of the College's Department of Administrative Engineering (later Industrial Engineering) and would receive a full salary of about $5,000, but would work only half time. (Coincidentally, Edwards Deming joined the NYU faculty just a year after Juran did, as professor of statistics at the Graduate School of Business Administration.)

To complement the teaching and writing, Juran added the third element of his pieced-together career: consulting. It would provide additional income, and—equally as important—experience, exposure, and knowledge. Management consulting was a burgeoning profession at the time, "booming as it never has before" according to a 1944 *Fortune* article which estimated that more than 1,200 consultants were operating in eight major U.S. cities, and that companies were spending some $65 million per year on advice. Newsletters providing specialized advice to managers and other professionals were proliferating, and advice could be bought on a variety of subjects, including organizational structure, incentives and compensation, distribution, line production, and strategy.

The consulting profession had been growing since before the turn of the century. Frederick W. Taylor (1856–1915) had followed a route similar to the one Juran had taken, starting as a shop-floor machinist and working his way up through management, until going freelance as a consultant, lecturer, and writer. Frank Gilbreth (1868–1924) worked, lectured, consulted, and wrote (although his books, including *Bricklaying System,* were narrowly focused), as did his wife and partner, Lillian (1878–1972). Henry L. Gantt (1861–1919), an associate of Taylor, became a consulting industrial engineer in 1901 and published more than 150 works including 3 major books, as well as lecturing at Harvard, Columbia, and Yale.

In addition to these independents, management consulting firms had taken root in the early part of the century. These firms generally began by offering a specific professional service, such as engineering or accounting consultation. Dr. Arthur Dehon Little was a professor at MIT when he founded his consulting firm in 1886. Edwin Booz (founder of the consultancy now known as Booz, Allen & Hamilton) established his firm in 1925 to provide market research and business studies. James McKinsey had been a professor of accounting when he began McKinsey & Company, in 1926. But, chastened by his less than satisfactory experience in large organizations, Juran had no interest in founding a consulting firm and growing a business; he wanted to be on his own, free of all the problems and frustrations of managing people. So, he struck a deal with a well-known management consultant of the day, Wallace Clark. Clark had been engaged since 1912 in the "installation of management methods" as he described it, and had gotten his start as an assistant to H. L. Gantt. Clark, also a successful writer, had popularized the Gantt Chart—Gantt's tool for time and project management—in a book called *The Gantt Chart, A Working Tool of Management,* published in 1922 and translated into eleven languages. Clark had developed a reputation as an expert on the flow of work (a term now generally streamlined into the simpler workflow) and specialized in bringing American methods to international business organizations. Prior to World War II, Clark had established offices in Paris and other European capitals. Among other successes, a *Fortune* article notes that "Clark was decorated for reorganizing Polish industry" and that he had "improved operation of the Turkish state monopolies of tobacco, salt, and alcohol." But, after the war, with the European economy devastated, Clark sought to expand his business in the United States. Clark agreed to hire Juran for consulting projects on a per-diem basis. At that time, rates for consultants generally fell in the range of $50 to $300 per day, depending on the experience of the person and the nature of the assignment, so the Clark connection offered Juran the greatest potential for income.

With the three essential pieces of his new life in place—writing, teaching, and consulting—Juran was ready to make the formal break with Western Electric. He wrote his letter of resignation on July 3, 1945. It is heavy on subtext and carefully written to avoid offense while providing as much explanation—with particular reference to the problem of anti-Semitism—as possible.

My dear Mr. Hosford:

I have accepted, as of September 1, 1945, the post of Chairman of the Department of Administrative Engineering at New York University. This action is a breach of the terms of my leave of absence, and constitutes a resignation from the Western Electric Company.

You must understand that it is no trivial reason which has caused me to break a tenure of over twenty-one years with the Bell System. For most of that time there existed, between a big corporation and an immigrant boy, a relationship which if it could be put into words, would be an eloquent testimonial to "The Land of Opportunity."

For that long relationship I am most grateful. In the Bell System I found opportunity for learning, for doing and for growing. I formed many enduring friendships. And I trust I contributed to the organization much more than I took out.

It is mainly because the road of opportunity has recently seemed for me to be approaching a barricade that I have concluded I should take another road. Why is there a barricade? It is all very complicated. Perhaps some day there will be less barricades, and less wars. But the barricade did seem to be there, and that is why I have taken a new road.

All this in no way detracts from my unbounded admiration of the Bell System as a foremost example of enlightened Big Business. Neither does it detract from my very real fondness for the integrity and the capability of the men of the Bell System. The problem which confronted me has its roots in the dim past, long before there was any Bell System. For that problem, there will be, even in my century, no complete solution.

My new duties will in time bring me in touch with many of those executives in the Metropolitan Area who are concerned with various aspects of Scientific Management. I am hopeful and quite confident that among these will be some of the Bell System executives.

May I, in any event, use this opportunity to renew my best good wishes to you and to all the others. All those years were not merely preparing for life; they were life itself. In that organization, and among those men, it was a very good way to live.

In all sincerity,

J. M. Juran

THE QUALITY COMMUNITY

Juran had joined Western Electric at the Hawthorne Works during a period of extraordinary growth and excitement, when enormous business energy was to be found in large factories, in the development of new quality methods, in experimentation with the organization of work processes, and in the shaping of management thinking. After the war, Juran again placed himself at a center of fervid business energy. With his new employer, his publisher, and his consulting associate all located in New York, it was necessary for the Jurans to move back to the New York area from Washington. To avoid travel problems, they chose a house in Westchester County, closer to Manhattan than their former residence in Summit, New Jersey had been. It was their third move in eight years.

In New York, Juran became a member of a loosely knit community of executives, engineers, writers, teachers, and consultants who were active in developing the field of management and quality methods. Much of the energy in the field came from the government's emphasis on quality methods for the production of equipment and matériel during World War II. The war effort was so great, the government had been pressed to find ways to ensure the quality of large batches of goods from a wide variety of suppliers—and to do it as quickly as possible. A group of statisticians at Stanford University believed that statistical methods could be of help. In 1942, one of the group, W. Allen Wallis, wrote to his friend Dr. W. Edwards Deming, who was then working at the Bureau of the Census. (Deming had developed sampling methods for the 1940 Census—the first one to use sampling methods to poll Americans on a variety of issues.) "Those of us teaching statistics in various departments here," wrote Wallis, "are trying to work out a curriculum adapted to the immediate statistical requirements of the war." Deming replied with a four-page letter. "There is no royal short-cut to producing a highly trained statistician," wrote Deming, "but I do firmly believe that the most important principles of application can be expounded in a very short time to engineers and others."

This exchange led to the development of a course on quality control, which Deming taught 23 times to small groups of engineers. Eventually the course was formalized into an eight-day session, and came under the sponsorship of the U.S. Office of Production Research and Development, part of the War Production Board, headed by Professor Holbrook Working of Stanford. Over a period of three years, from 1942–1945, the course reached some 31,000 students, including engineers, inspectors, and other personnel, many of them at companies involved in war production. The courses stimulated the founding of local quality societies, which eventually coalesced into a national organization, the American Society for Quality Control (ASQC), created in February 1946. The wartime courses and the resultant use of statistical tools not only contributed to the Allied victory, they "brought about a significant increase in the productivity of American industry," according to Wallis.

To businesspeople worldwide, the winning of the war came to be seen as a fabulous accomplishment of manufacture and management, as much as military might. Kaoru Ishikawa, Japan's leading quality proponent, states: "America's wartime production was quantitatively, qualitatively, and economically very satisfactory, owing in part to the introduction of statistical quality control, which also stimulated technological advances. One might even speculate that the Second World War was won by quality control and by the utilization of modern statistics." Peter Drucker agrees, asserting that the United States won the war "because of our productive capacity and our management ability, our ability to get supplies to any part of the world and coordinate them."

Management itself took on status as a profession, and American management, in particular, became regarded as the finest in the world. Peter Drucker, who, before the war, had written mostly about macroeconomic and societal issues, in 1954 wrote *The Practice of Management,* which he subtitled *A Study of the Most Important Function in American Society.* Juran, too, considered himself a student of general management, and directed some of his early efforts to exploring the broad management issues of strategy, finance, competition, and the role of the corporation in society. His first book, *Bureaucracy,* had taken a macro view of the organization. In 1948, he wrote an article for *Advanced Management* magazine called *Transition in Corporate Controls,* which discusses the emerging role of management as the policy-making function and trustee for company owners. But, with so much activity and demand coming from the burgeoning quality community, his focus gradually sharpened on the quality function and managing for quality.

In addition to his teaching duties—which included conducting accounting courses for engineering students, as well as his specialty, Management of Inspection and Quality Control—Juran busied himself with teaching and lecturing outside his commitments at NYU. Peter Drucker had joined the Business School faculty in 1950, at Juran's urging. Juran had read Drucker's early work, including *The End of Economic Man* and *The Future of the Industrial Man*. In the late 1940s, while on a trip to visit his son in camp, Juran had made a stop at Bennington College, in Vermont, where Drucker was teaching at the time. Juran called on Drucker, whom he had not met, and suggested that he was wasting his time in the remote village and ought to be teaching in the city. Soon enough, Drucker joined the faculty at NYU.

In 1946, Juran developed, in collaboration with Drucker, a management seminar that they called the Management Roundtable. "An elite corporal's guard of managers attended that pioneering event," Juran wrote in 1964. Juran served as moderator and principal speaker for the half-day Roundtable session, with Drucker following in the afternoon. While Drucker preferred a traditional lecture style, he recalls that Juran encouraged—perhaps provoked—participation in his segment of the course. "Nobody has ever accused him of being easygoing," says Drucker. "Juran made demands of the participants. Basically, he said, 'If you know what to do, why the hell don't you do it?'" The Roundtable became the model for a course Juran later conducted through the American Management Association, beginning in the early 1950s and continuing through the 1970s.

Even with all the activity in quality, the years of the late 1940s and 1950s were lean years for seminars on the *management* of Quality Control. "Instead, the train of Statistical Quality Control roared noisily down the track," wrote Juran. "Not only could nothing stop it;

nothing else could be heard above the roar." In other words, quality was considered to be the province of engineers and statisticians, not of managers. Changing this perception, and arguing the case for quality management, became a lifelong crusade for Juran—and others in the quality movement. In the late 1940s, as a speaker at a meeting of the metropolitan section of the ASQC, Juran chastised his audience—composed mostly of engineers—for their overreliance on technical tools and statistical methods. Those razzle-dazzle tools would not be useful in convincing senior managers to adopt quality methods, Juran told his listeners. Rather, he said, they should translate their message into the language that senior managers knew best—the language of finance. This would become a major theme for Juran throughout the years. Some members of the quality community "viewed Juran with caution" after that presentation, believes a longtime colleague.

THE HANDBOOK

Through his teaching, his speeches, his seminars, and his consulting assignments, Juran steadily refined his ideas, and began to shape them into what would become his third and breakthrough book, *Quality-Control Handbook*.

In 1945, Juran had signed a contract with the McGraw-Hill Book Company, (after being rejected by John Wiley & Sons and Macmillan), to produce a practical work on quality management and quality methods. He received no advance on royalties for the book, but plunged into the work that would take six years to complete. He began assembling material while still living in Washington, enlisting his wife and two older children to help. They would join him on Saturday mornings at the Library of Congress, and copy onto file cards, for later reference, the abstracts of books and articles that he wanted to pursue.

Juran intended his new work to be the first handbook in the field of quality control. He wished to make available, as he writes in the preface, "in ready reference form, the known principles and practices for achieving better quality at lower cost." The book, therefore, was not meant as a meditation or a theoretical work on the subject of quality. Juran wanted it to be the book on the shelf in the engineering cubicle, the manufacturing office and—he hoped—the executive suite. It would contain a number of articles, covering a wide range of topics. For those subjects in which he had insufficient expertise, he would enlist colleagues and known experts in the field as contributors.

Intent on keeping costs down and wanting to avoid creating a separate support organization, Juran went at his projects with the help of his wife and a few freelance collaborators. The result of conducting so much activity with so little infrastructure was a six-year prepublication period that began with his resignation from Western Electric in 1945 and ended with the publication of the *Handbook* in 1951 that Juran remembers as a time of "teetering." "As my consulting grew and as my fee scale rose commensurate with the deeds I was able to perform, we began to work our way out of the slim financial means which were plaguing us all the time. By the late 1940s we had two children in college and rising medical fees growing out of Bob's involvements. I was leading a harassed form of life due to the vicious multiple demands on my time—all that writing, the other hours needed to be invested for future returns, the long travel itineraries, the nights away from home, in poor hotels, on crowded trains, in airports, on noisy propeller-driven planes, driving long distances, etc. The budding consultant leads a dog's life from the standpoint of creature comforts and endures a good deal of pushing around by clients."

Wallace Clark, who had been Juran's major source of consulting assignments, died in 1948. Although Juran made an attempt to buy his business, he could not reach a deal with Clark's wife. But his own consulting business burgeoned, and, in 1950, due to the increasing pressure of work, and an increasingly unsatisfactory relationship with the Dean of the College of Engineering, Juran resigned his post at NYU. Whatever anxiety that decision may have caused was virtually erased with the publication of the *Handbook* in the spring of 1951— an 800-page, $10 volume packed with charts, descriptions of methods, case examples, studies, and references. Of its fifteen articles, Juran had written six himself.

One reviewer expressed the difference between this work and others in print at the time. "It is likely to be a revelation to anyone whose concept of quality control has been established on the comparative flood of books concerned with the techniques of statistical method in quality control. Dr. Juran tries to place the statistical techniques in their proper position within the overall quality function. There is a consistent emphasis throughout the book on the economic importance of quality control. Thus the viewpoint that quality control is concerned with establishing an overall program in which all departments participate recurs again and again throughout the book."

1951 was a banner year for quality-related publishing. Armand V. Feigenbaum published *Quality Control: Principles, Practice and Administration,* another heavy McGraw-Hill tome—with 443 pages and a steep $7 jacket price—and also a practical work that explored quality from the management perspective. John Wiley & Sons published W. Edwards Deming's book, *Some Theory of Sampling.* It was one of the first books to fully explore the theory of sampling and one reviewer predicted "it seems likely that for some time to come this book will be the 'bible' of sampling statisticians." *Some Theory* added another 600 pages to the literature.

On the lighter side, readers still remembered *Cheaper by the Dozen,* a best-seller of 1949, in which two of Frank and Lillian Gilbreth's twelve children told their family story. So, the subjects of business, quality, management, and consultants were well represented in both the technical and popular press. Even with a fair amount of competition, Juran's book quickly found an audience throughout the United States and around the world. It presented, in clear and accessible form, many of the key ideas that Juran would continue to enrich and embellish over the next five decades. Three of those ideas are worth reviewing here.

Prevent, Don't Inspect

It is not necessary to understand variation or statistics to understand that it makes more sense to produce something properly (whatever it is) than to make it incorrectly and then fix it or throw it away. Twenty-year-old Inspector J. M. Juran could plainly see the problem at the Hawthorne Works. He spent his days dashing around the plant finding, fixing, rectifying, or scrapping things that were not right. And he was just one of 5,000 inspectors who, in 1924, busily inspected materials, components, assembled products, and field installations—to find mistakes, catch errors, remove problems, and make sure bad product didn't go out the door. Some twenty years later, in 1946, The Gillette Company—one of Juran's earliest clients—faced the same problem. And, today, at factory after factory, white-coated inspectors hover near the end of a production line, earnestly weeding out the bad and blessing the good.

Often, a young person, a new hire, coming into an industrial organization with fresh eyes will notice that the system seems ineffectual and wrongheaded. If bold and bright enough, he or she will comment, "This is crazy! Why do we do it this way?" Sometimes, such a comment will provoke a change initiative. Most often, it will provoke a resigned answer to the effect, "I know, but that's how it works." Juran comments that although Hawthorne was chaotic, it was a chaos that everyone in the plant understood and that, after all, produced a remarkable product for its day.

So, a question lies at the heart of quality: "Wouldn't it be better, simpler, cheaper, and smarter to *prevent* mistakes and defects, rather than remove them once they have occurred? Doesn't a product that is built or assembled properly from the beginning generally look and perform better than one that has been reworked?" And, of course, the answer is yes.

The Juran family, photographed in Romania, 1910, not long before they left for America to join Jakob. Left to Right: Nathan, Rudy, Joseph, Gitel, and Rebecca.

The first Juran home in America, 3445 Central Avenue in Minneapolis, where all eight family members lived in three rooms, without electricity, heat, or plumbing, circa 1912.

Joseph M. Juran, age 18, from the University of Minnesota publication "Gopher."

$$x = ?$$

Wanted–
men to find the answer

THIS is written to the man who loves to seek the unknown quantity. He is the kind of laboratory worker who ventures into untried fields of experiment, rather than the man who tests materials.

Industry has need of both types, but of the former there is a more pressing demand.

College men may have been discouraged from pursuing pure research. In this highly practical age it may seem there is little room for work which does not have an immediate dollars and cents application. But such is not the case.

The pure research man is the pathfinder. Without him our fountain of knowledge would dry up. His findings in themselves may be uncommercial, but they establish a field for others to develop.

Volta worked out the crude voltaic pile—unimportant until other men improved and applied it. And so with Papin in the field of steam, or Lavoisier in chemistry.

Men of the inquiring slant of mind, stick to your last. In post graduate study, on the faculty, in the laboratory of some industrial organization, there will always be an "X" to baffle other men and call for the keenest thought of you blazers of the trail.

Published in the interest of Electrical Development by an Institution that will be helped by whatever helps the Industry.

Western Electric Company

Since 1869 makers and distributors of electrical equipment

Number 29 of a series

A Western Electric recruiting advertisement that ran in a 1923 issue of *Technolog,* a student publication of the College of Engineering at the University of Minnesota. Juran interviewed with Western Electric, Western Union, and General Electric. (Reprinted by permission of the Institute of Technology Board of Publications, University of Minnesota.)

Quitting time at Western Electric's Hawthorne Works, Chicago, circa 1928. Most workers commuted by foot or streetcar but the streets were increasingly jammed with automobiles, as well. (Property of AT&T Archives. Reprinted with permission of AT&T.)

A coil winder at the Hawthorne Works. This might have been one of the young women involved in the Hawthorne experiments which were among the earliest explorations of the human issues involved in factories and mass production. (Property of AT&T Archives. Reprinted with permission of AT&T.)

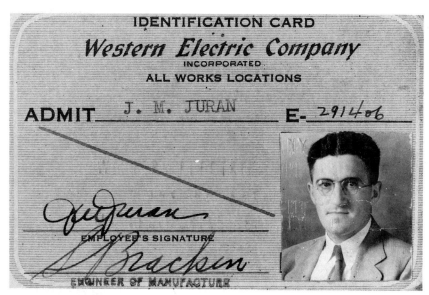

Juran's identification card at Hawthorne Works. He started in the Inspection Branch in 1924 and worked in a variety of engineering and management positions until 1937, when he was promoted to Western Electric headquarters in New York City.

Juran visited Japan for the first time in 1954 where he conducted a number of lectures and seminars on quality management.

Juran received the National Medal of Technology in 1992 from President Bush, "for providing the key principles and methods by which enterprises manage the quality of their products and processes."

The impulse can lend itself to facile sloganeering. ("Do it right the first time!" "Zero defects.") But it is hellishly difficult and complicated—especially within a large, industrial organization that makes complex, precision products—to implement and achieve the desired result.

Two Facets of Quality

Prevention of defects is only half of the quality story. Even if a producer of manufactured goods or of services could achieve perfection—no defects in manufacture, 100 percent conformance to specifications, no failures in performance—the product still might not be of use to anyone. Or it might not be as useful as a competitive product. Or it simply might not appeal to the customer. In other words, achieving defect-free manufacture of a useless or unsalable product would be futile and absurd. So, quality also implies customer acceptance and usefulness.

But, especially in the early days of quality consciousness, the notion of customer acceptance was a source of confusion to many people; they equated quality with worth or luxury, or what Juran calls "grade." Walter Shewhart was among the first to attack what he perceived to be the popular conception, or misconception, of quality. He wrote, in 1939, "Dating at least from the time of Aristotle, there has been some tendency to conceive of quality as indicating the *goodness* of an object. The majority of advertisers appeal to the public upon the basis of the quality of product. In so doing, they implicitly assume that there is a measure of goodness which can be applied to all kinds of product whether it be vacuum tubes, sewing machines, automobiles, Grape Nuts, books, cypress flooring, Indiana limestone, or correspondence school courses. Such a concept, is, however, too indefinite for practical purposes."

Shewhart then argued that the quality of anything is not about some intangible, unknowable goodness—the "soul" of a product. "Quality," he wrote, "in Latin *qualitas,* comes from *qualis,* meaning

'how constituted' and signifies such as the thing really is." To Shewhart, therefore, a product was a constitution of characteristics that can
be defined and measured. Shewhart was a physicist and engineer; he
had a scientist's perspective. A marketing or advertising person might
argue that, in fact, a constitution of product characteristics adds up to
something more, an intangible essence that cannot really be measured.
Is a Coke just a syrup formula and a bottle shape? Is a Mercedes a set
of tolerances? Is a software program nothing more than its lines of
code? Product designers and manufacturing personnel, however, must
deal with tangibles.

Juran addressed this aspect of quality in the first edition of the
Handbook. "The elemental building block out of which 'quality' is
constructed is the *quality characteristic*. A physical or chemical property,
a dimension, a temperature, a pressure, or any other requirement used
to define the nature of a product or a service is a quality characteristic." He then went on to differentiate between the two aspects of quality, which he called quality of design and quality of conformance.
Quality of design, he said, has to do with "a variation in specification
for the same functional use." As illustration, Juran offered automobiles. A Cadillac, he said, has a higher quality of design; a Chevrolet
has a lower quality of design. He was talking here about the importance of the customer aspect of quality. At the same time, this definition allows the reader to make the mistake of equating quality with
luxury.

Juran then addressed the second aspect of quality—quality of
conformance. Conformance, he said, relates to the "fidelity with
which the product *conforms* to the design. A Chevrolet that can run
and a Chevrolet which cannot run have the same quality of design,
but they differ in quality of conformance." What he didn't say, in
1951, was that the defect-free Chevrolet and the defect-free Cadillac meet specific customer needs and, therefore, can be considered of
equal quality.

Over the years, Juran refined his definitions, while retaining the
two essential aspects:

1. Quality consists of those product features that meet the needs of customers and thereby provide product satisfaction.
2. Quality consists of freedom from deficiencies.

The term *product satisfaction* avoids the association of quality with "worth" or "grade" or "luxury." It tells us that a Chevrolet, or any product, so long as it successfully meets customer needs and is free of problems, is a quality product. This bifurcated definition seems a simplistic statement of a complex phenomenon. But, like any good definition, it tends to effectively corral a limitless number of questions toward a limited number of answers, and it provides a useful way to understand quality for people at all levels within an organization.

Juran, when asked to simplify, combines the two definitions into the phrase "fitness for use."

The Cost of Quality

Both aspects of quality have an impact on the financial health of a producing organization. Reduce defects, eliminate waste, cut the amount of rework, inspect less—all these activities serve to reduce costs. For the most part, the process of finding and effecting these cost reductions does not require an outlay of capital. Over the decades, company after company has realized significant cost savings without buying any new equipment or adding any staff. Juran wrote that "higher quality of conformance generally costs less" than low quality of conformance, because the resources expended will be less than the savings gained. He referred to this phenomenon as "gold in the mine"—money that already exists within an organization and simply has to be dug out. It is this aspect of quality that Philip Crosby celebrates in his slogan (and the title of his best-selling book, published in 1980) *Quality Is Free*. However, there is a limit, because the closer a company comes to achieving zero defectives, the more the effort will cost (see Figure 4.1). Eventually, it will be more expensive to reduce

Figure 4.1 The cost of quality control climbs steeply as the number of defects nears zero. This offsets the cost savings achieved through control, and causes the total cost of manufacturing to rise. (From J. M. Juran, *Quality Control Handbook* (1st ed.), 1951. New York: McGraw-Hill. Reproduced with permission of McGraw-Hill Companies.)

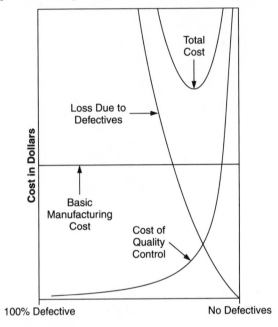

defects than to live with them. It will become just too difficult to find and extract every nugget of gold in the mine.

In contrast to quality *conformance,* which generally reduces the cost of manufacture, achievement of a higher-level quality of *design*—adding features that increase customer satisfaction—generally will increase costs, explains Juran. To determine what features and characteristics should be developed, determine the best way to produce them, and develop a process that will enable the producer to make them without defects—these activities can consume a great deal of resources. "The basic quality problem," Juran explains, "is to strike the correct balance between cost of quality and value of quality for each quality characteristic."

ASSIGNMENT: GILLETTE

Juran's essential message—it was better to prevent defects rather than inspect them out of the process—was an enormously powerful one for his clients. One of his first was The Gillette Company, the maker of blades and razors, based in Boston. For a decade, Gillette had been stung by criticism of the quality of its blades. In 1932, the company had felt the need to run full-page newspaper ads that apologized for the substandard quality of a new product, the Kroman De Luxe blade. Other blade and razor makers suffered similar quality problems, but Gillette prided itself on its manufacturing, and wished to set the industry standard for blade quality.

Criticism also came from within the company. In the mid 1930s, Gillette's manufacturing facility in Great Britain had complained about the quality of the products produced by the South Boston plant. Eventually, the British convinced the Americans to replace the equipment in one of the key manufacturing steps, blade sharpening, with a British machine, known as the Green Demon. Disposing of the old machines caused a problem; Gillette worried that competitors might get hold of the equipment and learn the proprietary manufacturing techniques.

When Juran came on the scene at Gillette, in 1946, he not only faced onerous quality problems there, he also encountered a culture highly resistant to change. The workforce had resisted the suggestions from their British colleagues; they were even more suspicious of outsiders brought in to improve products that were considered to be the finest blades and razors in the world. Howard Gambrill, Gillette's head of manufacturing, helped set up a small quality team in the razor division. Leonard Seder, who would later contribute to Juran's *Handbook* and join Juran on the seminar circuit, was brought in from General Electric to help. During World War II, Seder had taken the eight-day course offered by the War Production Board, and applied what he had learned with success—significantly raising the yield of GE's products essential to the war effort.

Juran suggested that they start with a pilot project on a screw machine that produced most of the important parts of the razor. (In Gillette parlance, the razor is the handle of the shaving device.) If the project proved successful, the team would tackle additional razor improvement projects.

At the time, losses from scrap and rework at the screw machines were so considerable that Gillette employed a force of twenty-five bench inspectors, along with several roving inspectors, to watch over the output of fifty machines. Gillette had already engaged in several "fact finding" programs to determine the cause of the problem, but had failed to come up with anything more than educated guesses.

Juran set about the project methodically. The team analyzed inspection data regarding defect, rework, and rejection rates of the screw machines. They translated that information into cost data—how much money was being lost—and performed a Pareto Analysis to determine which defects would contribute the greatest savings, if discovered and rectified. They then set about tackling those "vital few" defects, one at a time. On the factory floor, Seder studied and analyzed the operations, often with the help of new measuring instruments and tools. With the assistance of the machine operators, he was able to determine the causes of the defects. Juran focused on analyzing Seder's data, and explaining the findings to management.

As one machine after another produced more and more acceptable product, the team took their methods and message to the rest of the personnel. They conducted training sessions for the foremen and machine operators, in which they explained the concepts of variation and control and taught them how to use simple control charts. By involving the workers, Juran and his team transformed their initial skepticism into interest and, eventually, into enthusiasm.

As the recommended changes took effect, improvements to the quality of the razor swiftly followed. At the start of the project, around Thanksgiving, the defect rate was about 20 percent. By mid-December, the rate had plummeted to 7 percent. By mid–March, 1947, Gillette was able to eliminate routine bench inspections for the razor part, and 100 percent inspection had become a relic of the past.

To implement similar changes throughout the plant, Juran had to win over Gillette management, a victory he accomplished by convincing Gambrill, the manufacturing chief, of the potential for cost savings through quality improvement. By the end of 1947, Juran had analyzed and revamped the manufacture of every part in a Gillette razor. In one year, Juran and his young Quality Department had reduced the cost of manufacturing razors by one-third. The inspection force was reduced from twenty-five to just one. When that lonely inspector was pictured in a *Fortune* Magazine article, Gillette's public relations people fretted that readers would think Gillette cared little about quality.

Both management and the workers were pleased with Juran's work. A survey of machine operators revealed that four out of five of the workers believed that the quality control charts provided them with a better understanding of their jobs. Nine out of ten thought the charts gave them the power to improve the quality of their work. On the lecture circuit, Gillette's senior managers expressed their delight with the results. In 1949, in a dinner address to the Boston Chapter of the ASQC, Gillette President Joseph Spang told his audience, "By the middle of 1948, our costs from spoilage, rework, and inspection were cut by 76 percent. Translated into dollars, that 76 percent became a figure that I can assure you was most impressive." Spang also praised "the boost in morale of employees which comes with the installation of quality methods."

Juran continued to work with Gillette into the early 1950s. He would take the train from New York to Boston, there dividing his time between the Quality Department and senior managers. His resounding success with razors led to similar work on blades, and later, when Gillette was developing its first shaving test room, he was invited by Meyer Shnitzler, head of R&D (and a friend), to establish the statistical foundation for understanding shaving test results. This shaving test room would play an important role in the development of Gillette's product breakthroughs over the next decade.

Juran's contribution to Gillette lay as much in his ability to influence the culture—both on the factory floor and in the executive offices—as it did in the reduction of waste and, thus, of cost. Gillette was still operating largely according to the rule-of-thumb methods that had prevailed prior to Taylor and his scientific principles of management. Juran fostered a willingness to challenge traditional approaches with scientific analysis and to give workers more responsibility. Juran's contemporaries remember his forcefulness as both a teacher and an implementer of quality methods.

Thanks to Juran's contribution, Gillette could more confidently assert that it was the shaving leader and that it offered blades and razors of the highest, most consistent quality. Never again did Gillette feel the need to issue an apology for poor quality.

For Juran, the swift and demonstrable success at Gillette—a reduction in defects and a concomitant reduction in costs, and a change in culture—boosted his reputation and helped him capture further consulting assignments.

5

Children of
the Occupation
(1954)

Juran's inspiration was like welcome rain.

William Tsutsui

MYTH

In the past two decades or so, an appealing myth has emerged about the role played by Americans in shaping the rebuilding of postwar Japanese industry. According to the myth, a handful of American experts gallantly galloped into war-ravaged Japan, with W. Edwards Deming as the intellectual hero leading the charge (see Figure 5.1). These experts possessed a complete and intimate knowledge of the principles and practices of management that had enabled America to win the war and become the world's greatest industrial producer. The beleaguered and benighted Japanese managers received this wisdom with infinite gratitude and immediately set about applying it. Meanwhile, American managers gradually "forgot" their own principles, and grew ever more arrogant, inflexible, and complacent. Japanese

Figure 5.1 Deming first visited Japan in 1947. Juran's first visit was in 1954.

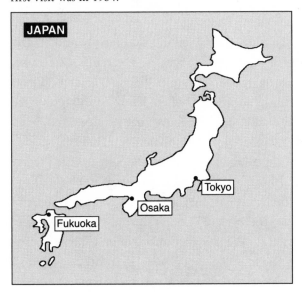

companies beavered busily away until, at last, in the 1970s, they rose to the point where they could challenge and beat U.S. companies, on American turf. Awakening as if from an enchanted sleep in the early 1980s, American managers scrambled to learn and apply Japanese management principles and play catch-up. Then, come to find out, those Japanese principles weren't truly Japanese at all; they were actually American ideas in Japanese clothing. O, the irony! Why hadn't we done as the Japanese had done? Why hadn't our managers listened? How could we have been so blind, so stupid? Only in the 1990s, as Japanese industry experienced a variety of problems and American industry grew both leaner and stronger, did we cease to berate ourselves and to exalt the Japanese.

The myth about the American role in creating the Japanese "miracle" endures because it is a compelling story that contains a quantity of truth, and because it has been colorfully promulgated by some of its leading characters, most notably Deming himself. Lloyd Dobyns and Clare Crawford-Mason—creators of *If Japan Can . . . Why Can't We?*, the NBC broadcast that brought Deming into national awareness— describe a Deming dinner party they attended in the mid-1980s. "Pressed to say what had made the difference in Japan, a question he had always avoided, Deming drew himself to his full seated height, slapped his hand on the table, and said firmly and finally, 'One lone man with profound knowledge.'"—referring, of course, to himself. Perhaps Deming was engaging in his self-described propinquity for always providing an answer when asked an intriguing question; perhaps he truly had come to believe that he alone had made the difference in Japan. But it would be difficult to find many observers—even among Deming disciples—who would agree with the assertion.

In fact, although Japanese industry was in chaos after the war—as a result of a defeated national strategy, physical devastation, and a lack of leadership—there were enough business leaders who could analyze the situation and take steps to improve it. One of these steps was to seek help, in the form of expert advice, from the world's best business advisers. At that time, America was the strongest economy on earth and the greatest producer of manufactured goods, so the Japanese naturally looked to us for help—despite the disturbing fact that America was also Japan's recent military conqueror. The Japanese did not listen to American experts only in the seminar rooms of Tokyo, Osaka, and Fukuoka. They traveled to the United States, visited factories, and talked with American managers, to see firsthand how it was done. For example, Eiji Toyoda, of The Toyota Motor Company, studied Ford's River Rouge plant in the spring of 1950. And they looked beyond the United States as well, sending delegations to other industrialized countries to study their methods and management practices. In short, there was far more exposure to and exchange of ideas in postwar Japan than Deming's pronouncement would lead one to imagine.

BEHIND THE MYTH

Deming was not the first American to talk to the Japanese about quality and business management. The stream of U.S. experts into Japan had begun in the early years of the Occupation and General Douglas MacArthur, at General Headquarters of the Supreme Commander for the Allied Powers (SCAP), had primed the pump.

When MacArthur arrived in Japan, in August 1945, he wanted to communicate with the Japanese people to reassure them that the occupying forces meant no harm and to help them understand the mission of SCAP. He assigned the task of Japan-wide communication to Civil Information and Education Section (CI&E), an agency within his headquarters, but CI&E had no means of mass communication at its disposal. Most of the printing presses had been destroyed, virtually no Japanese had radios in their homes, and television, of course, had yet to come into general use. The telephone system was similarly in disarray. Throughout Japan, phone lines often jangled with noise or went suddenly dead. For Americans, used to a coast-to-coast telephone network that performed splendidly for the most part, the Japanese system was unacceptable. But, at the time, the American policy was that the Japanese would have to support themselves—there would be no importation into Japan of funds or materials from the United States. So, Japanese industry would have to be mobilized to manufacture the equipment required for communication, including home radio receivers and telephones.

In September 1945, Homer Sarasohn, a 29-year old electronics expert, was working at the Raytheon Company when he received a telegram from a colonel in Washington that read, "General MacArthur's headquarters has requested your services at the earliest possible date." Many youthful pranksters were working with Sarasohn, so he figured it was a joke—until the colonel called him on the telephone a couple of weeks later and bawled him out for ignoring the telegram. Sarasohn agreed to journey to Washington to talk with the colonel and, soon after, he was on his way to Japan.

Sarasohn had received a BS in physics and chemistry from Wayne University in Detroit, and had done some graduate work at the RCA Institute in what then was called radio engineering, but would now be considered electronics. Lacking the funds to finish his PhD, he went to work for the Crosley Corporation (where, incidentally, Philip Crosby, author of *Quality Is Free* later worked, starting in 1952), specializing in high-powered radio transmitters and radio detection and ranging (radar) systems. Crosley asked him to design a home radio receiver, which he did. "They patted me on the top of my pointed little head and the marketing guy said, 'Oh, that's a terrific job you've done. Now take it back and redesign it so it'll sell for $19.95.' And that made me angry, so I quit, because I didn't like that crass commercialism."

After a brief stint at a manufacturer of test equipment, Sarasohn was discontented again and decided—although the nature of his work (and his Quaker religion) exempted him from the draft—to request that his draft board ignore his deferment. So the Army happily drafted him, in mid-1943, and he reported to Fort Collins, Colorado, for duty in the 161st Airborne Engineers. But he brought his plane down heavy one day, and he was mustered out of the Army with a medical discharge. He was asked to join the Radiation Laboratory at MIT. His job was to take prototypes of airborne radar systems from the lab, and get them into commercially viable form as swiftly as possible. Sarasohn proved to be adept at this and one of the systems he helped bring out of the lab—then called the Cadillac system—is still in use as AWACS (Airborne Warning and Control System). So, Sarasohn had expertise not only in radio systems but, equally important, in managing the process of rapid transition from laboratory prototype to production model—an expertise that MacArthur urgently required in Japan.

In early 1946, Sarasohn boarded a twin-engine, propeller-driven military aircraft and set off on a five day journey that took him from Cambridge, Massachusetts to an Air Force base in California, and then island-hopping across the Pacific to Tokyo. He reported for work to SCAP headquarters, in a six-story building that had been the home of the Dai Ichi ("Number One") insurance company and stood directly across the street from the Imperial Palace. Sarasohn's office was on the third floor, MacArthur's was on the sixth. "You are halfway to heaven!," one of his Japanese visitors remarked.

Sarasohn joined the Civil Communication Section (CCS) of the SCAP. One of his colleagues—"the telephone guy"—was Wilbur Magil, an engineer from Western Electric who had been at the Hawthorne Works with Juran in the 1920s. Magil had already begun working with Japanese manufacturers, including Nippon Electric Company (NEC), which had been established in 1899 as a joint venture between a group of Japanese investors and Western Electric. According to Koji Kobayashi, who was then general manager of the largest NEC plant in the Tokyo area and later became NEC chairman, NEC was founded to "absorb some of the technologies of Western Electric, which had the most advanced communications technology in the world."

But, admits Kobayashi, "The quality of our products at the time of postwar confusion was, quite frankly, terrible, partly because we could not obtain good materials." Even during the war, NEC's quality had been shockingly poor. "I remember that the yield of vacuum tubes for aircraft was one percent," writes Kobayashi. And, although NEC engineers had taken various steps to improve quality, they could not get around the prevailing management policy, which was "One tube today rather than ten tubes tomorrow." In fact, the quality of much Japanese-produced war equipment was uneven. There had been successes, most notably the Zero fighter aircraft, manufactured by Mitsubishi. But Takashi Kayano, now a consultant, remembers that some Japanese-made machine guns weren't much better than the vacuum tubes. "The machine gun wouldn't function many times, so you wouldn't be able to continue shooting. And so three people would share one small machine gun. One would shoot, one would load the gun, and the other one would stand by with a screwdriver to remove the bullet that got stuck in the gun."

One day, Magil called Kobayashi and asked him to come to his office at General Headquarters. Kobayashi remembered that the conversation "went something like this: that the Allied Forces were worried about public peace and order in Japan, and that the major weakness in the system was the poor quality of the communications networks; that unless NEC, which was a major supplier of communications equipment, could produce quality products at the earliest time, the occupation policy could not be performed smoothly; that NEC should practice quality control by all means, and that if I was interested he would help me." Magil did help NEC, according to Kobayashi. Although the company had some knowledge of quality control, "we restudied quality control under Magil's guidance. We first applied it to the production of vacuum tubes and we obtained remarkable results."

When he arrived, Sarasohn was given similar responsibilities to those of Magil. First, he was to help reestablish the telephone, telegraph, and radio broadcast systems throughout the country. Second, he was to get radio receivers into the hands of the public. One reason for building the communication infrastructure was that MacArthur wished to be able to speak directly with the Japanese people. The message, says Sarasohn, was simple, "The war's over. We're at peace.

We're not going to attack you, you don't have to attack us. You're going to have a new life. Yes, you will get fed." But MacArthur's communication with the general public was minimal; he primarily needed the telephone system to keep in contact with members of the Japanese government.

Sarasohn's third task was to help the Japanese rebuild the communications industry as a major component of the reestablishment of the economic life of the country. This came as the result of a decision—hotly debated at the highest levels of the U.S. government—that the Japanese should be allowed to rebuild their industries, rather than be kept subservient to the occupation force. Sarasohn "figured that if I could get factories in the position of being able to produce the radio equipment and the telephone equipment, then the third task would be accomplished and I would be working toward getting the first done."

But in Japan, Sarasohn had no MIT laboratory to develop prototypes, nor any Crosley factory within which to produce commercial product. When he arrived in Japan, "you could stand in Tokyo and if your eyesight were good enough you could look across the fields all the way down to Yokohama," more than twenty miles to the south. The area between Tokyo and Yokohama, once one of Japan's major industrial areas, had been completely wiped out by fire bombs and explosives. Factories lay in rubble. Machinery had been burned, exploded, or moved into the relative safety of the countryside. Workers, too, had gone into military service or fled into the country. The infrastructure was in disrepair. Train service was as unreliable as the phone service. Goods moved, *when* they moved, via three-wheeled vehicles or banged-up bicycles along ruined roads. Only about 41,000 motor vehicles were still functioning to serve the country's 70 million people on Japan's four islands—or, about 1,700 people per truck, car, or motorized bike. The Japanese merchant fleet had been devastated. As a result, industrial output just after the war stood at only 20 percent of its wartime peak, and at about 24 percent of its previous high, reached in 1934. In addition, the chronic, decades-long problems of Japanese industry had not

disappeared. Japan was—and still is—a resource-poor nation, short on
the raw materials that feed its industrial activities. At the war's end,
some 80 percent of its food came from outside Japan.

"It was difficult to know where to start and what to start with,"
remembers Sarasohn. Besides, neither the Americans nor the Japanese
knew what to expect from one another. "We were considered the dev-
ils from across the Pacific. They didn't know who we were, what we
were. We didn't know either. We expected, as in the Philippines and
Guadalcanal, that retribution would be visited upon us." Sarasohn,
like many other foreigners, arrived with a defensive attitude; he
walked around the city carrying a gun. "When I walked down the
street in Tokyo, I would set a course for myself straight ahead and
whoever was in my way got shoved out of my path. I was embittered
with anger and I hated the Japanese for what they had done, not only
to the Allied troops, but for the treatment of the Korean people and
the Korean comfort women." But, after about a month of acting as the
angry young American, Sarasohn had a change of attitude. "I was
walking down the street and all of a sudden I stopped and a light
turned on in my head. I said, 'Hey, with this attitude, I'm not going
to accomplish the job I'm here to do. This is not being constructive.'
I went through a metamorphosis."

Sarasohn and a colleague, Gilbert Weeks (who had replaced
Magil), set to work in earnest—Sarasohn assessing the state of the
radio industry, Weeks focusing on telephones. They found a broad
disparity in the sophistication and organization of the Japanese manufacturing operations. Many of the workshops were just plain dirty,
Sarasohn discovered. "They would have a man with some strips of
cloth tied to a handle which he whisked over the benches. I think his
job was to keep the atmosphere dusty." Sarasohn visited another small
company in the Shinagawa section of Tokyo. "Its listed capital was
$600; the minuscule staff were housed in shabby shacks where in a
rainstorm, executives had to work with umbrellas over their desks."
This was the company that would become Sony; Akio Morita was one
of the executives toiling under an umbrella.

Sarasohn and his colleagues began building and rebuilding factories from the ground up. "We cleared out areas where you could set up a shack and we went out looking for equipment that could be brought back and refurbished or repaired." They made connections with Japanese companies, including Matsushita and NEC, that had had good reputations as pre-war manufacturers of products related to radio manufacture, such as cable and copper wire. Many companies had operations and facilities outside the major cities, where little or no damage had been suffered. Working with the Eighth Army, which had installations throughout Japan, Sarasohn began to scrounge up raw materials and machines. He located wire-winding machines and evacuation devices to make vacuum tubes, then the heart of the radio. He even came across a vacuum tube assembly machine, which had been purchased from Western Electric before the war, and stood, unwrapped and untouched, at one factory site.

PURGE

The physical devastation faced by the Japanese, and by the CCS staff, was only the most tangible aspect of the state of crisis in Japanese industry. The human infrastructure had been equally devastated. The most obvious and disturbing fact was that so many people who had been—or could have been—industrial workers or business managers were dead: 2,300,000 men had been killed or wounded in battle; 800,000 civilians had been killed or injured at home. Many had starved to death after the war. Thousands more were prisoners of war in Russia.

In addition, MacArthur had ordered the dissolution of the dominating organizations of Japanese industry—the *zaibatsu* ("wealthy clique"). These were the great, family-controlled industrial networks of companies that had been the bedrock of Japanese industry since well before the turn of the century. The big four *zaibatsu* were Mitsui,

Mitsubishi, Sumitomo, and Yasuda. Their senior executives were forced to resign their positions, on the theory that they had been instrumental in the war effort and could not be trusted to cooperate in making the peace. Top executives from some 240 companies dependent on the *zaibatsu* were also banned from working for their companies for ten years. Another 250 companies were forced to retire their top managers. According to one estimate, a total of some 3,600 people were removed from the ranks of senior management between 1946 and 1948. Younger managers—many of them from functional positions in manufacturing, engineering, sales—were abruptly promoted into strategic decision-making positions. One Japanese executive confided to an American visitor that, before the war, he had been far down in the organizational hierarchy but that he had been thrust to the top during the Purge because everyone above him had been declared a war criminal.

As Peter Drucker, the business writer, puts it, "I think it's almost impossible to realize how fragile that society was, how close to the abyss of social disintegration it was. The old leadership was discredited, not just purged. The new people knew that the ways they had grown up with no longer worked. They were desperate, and very receptive, when American industry and American management were the models."

The situation thrust Sarasohn into the role of king-maker. "My experience was that the senior managers were put out of their jobs. The problem for me was, if I'm going to start Nippon Denki again, who will I have run the company? So what I did was reach in and take somebody whom I did not know and say to them, 'Now you're going to be the plant manager of the Kawasaki plant,' or whatever it was." Sarasohn believed that the best people to take over the reins of the ruined Japanese communications companies were engineers—not attorneys or accountants—so those were the people he chose. But, even with people with technical backgrounds, communication was difficult. In addition to the language barrier, the Japanese did not appear to understand many of Sarasohn's ideas.

By the middle of 1946, however, some progress had been made. Sarasohn gathered several plant managers in his office in the Dai Ichi building and told them: "We've got a plant built here and there. We've got machines working. We can operate them at least two hours a day, when we have electric power available. But we have problems. And I want you to tell me, from your point of view, what you think the major problem is that we should be aware of and we should make plans to deal with." The plant managers huddled together in the back of the room and deliberated so long that Sarasohn got irritated. He asked the interpreter what they were talking about, and he was told, "They're talking about what answer they should give you that will make you happy." Sarasohn, frustrated and determined to make a real connection with the Japanese, decided "right then and there that I was going to learn as much of the Japanese language and culture and mentality as I could so I could deal with these people." Within six months, he had a reasonable speaking capability and, during his five years in Japan, he learned to think in the Japanese language, as well.

SEMINAR

In 1948, Charles W. Protzman, a seasoned engineer who had joined Western Electric in 1922 (two years before Juran), came to Japan to work with Sarasohn in the Civil Communication Section (CCS). Together, Protzman and Sarasohn concluded that the central problem with the Japanese manufacturers was now not one of engineering, but of management. "They were very competent engineers and needed little or no technical advice," recalls Protzman. "What I did find was that they did not understand and apply the systems and routines of production management. Within a month of arriving in Japan, I had concluded that rather than try to correct each company individually, we should present a set of seminars on the principles of industrial management for top company executives."

Their immediate supervisor, however, did not agree. But, in June 1949, he was replaced by Frank Polkinghorn, another alumnus of AT&T—specifically, Bell Laboratories. He quickly approved the idea, and Protzman and Sarasohn set about creating a seminar to be called *Industrial Management*. They hastily developed a 357-page text in English, and also had it translated into a 488-page Japanese version. They then invited—perhaps "commanded" would be a more accurate word—the managers of the important communications companies to attend. With little initial enthusiasm, nineteen company presidents and executive directors attended the conference held in Tokyo (at Waseda University, starting September 26), and twenty-five more attended a session in the city of Osaka. They were the senior managers of the now-familiar names in the Japanese electronics industry: Masaharu Matsushita from Matsushita, Takeo Kato of Mitsubishi, Bunzaemon Inouye of Sumitomo, as well as representatives from NEC, Fujitsu, Toshiba, Hitachi, Sharp (then Hayakawa), Furukawa, Sumitomo Electric, and Oki. Six academics also attended, including Kaoru Ishikawa, who would become Japan's leading exponent of quality control. Both seminars ran eight weeks, four afternoons a week from 1 P.M. to 5 P.M. Sarasohn conducted his segments of the course in Japanese.

The *Industrial Management* text attempts to provide a complete overview of the modern (American) industrial organization and the principles of scientific management, and does so in a practical, straightforward, often elementary way. It is divided into four sections: I. Policy; II. Organization; III. Controls; IV. Operation. The text begins with a discussion of the importance of "making a clear statement of the objective of the enterprise," which the authors liken to "providing a target for a man shooting an arrow with a bow." A crude drawing supports this idea: a stick man labeled "Management" (misspelled) is aiming an arrow labeled "Company Efforts and Resources" at the target, labeled "Objective of the Enterprise."

The course then explores policy and policy enforcement, and provides examples of policies for sales, personnel, and public relations departments. In a section called "Design of Organization—Scientific

Approach," Sarasohn and Protzman provide some advice for setting up a factory. "If you are going to construct a factory building in which to manufacture a product you do not simpley [sic] go to a building [they meant, presumably, a builder] and say: 'I want you to construct a factory building for me. I am going to manufacture a product.' You are interested in other things than just a roof and walls, and a floor. The building is going to cost a lot of money to construct. You will expect to use it for a long time and it must be adequate for your needs. Then what do you do?"

After a discussion of the various forms of organization (which are defined as line, line and staff, functional) and how to construct them, Sarasohn and Protzman analyze the organization of an unnamed Japanese company. The company employs, they write, 7,000 people, in a headquarters building, eight branch offices, and eighteen factories. (A larger company than one might expect to find operating in 1948.) No company manual exists that describes the company's organization or the role of each position within it; only "some sheets of paper upon which are written some vague and inconclusive statements." Furthermore, all authority is wielded by the senior managers, but they are stretched extremely thin. Only a handful of people at the top are responsible for overseeing a large number of disparate departments, with a great number of direct reports. "It is a physical impossibility for any manager to adequately supervise such a multitude of different activities as is being demanded of these management people." Sarasohn and Protzman then address the ill effect of this management situation on the middle managers and workers:

> If the top executives reserve for themselves all the decisions that could be made at lower levels, if the people in the lower levels are not given a chance to act on their own authority, if they have no opportunity to develop their own executive abilities, they are going to lose interest in their jobs and if they don't leave the company to get better jobs, they will remain and do only mediocre work. They will have lost all their inspiration and incentive to extend their efforts to do better than just average work.

It is this extra margin of effort which so often spells the difference
between profit and loss, between a successful happy company and
a dispirited, falling-apart, failure of a company.

The course proceeds in this way, combining broad discussion
about the nature and design of large industrial organizations, with extensive detail about operational methods—down to a job description
of the janitor ("directs the cleaning and sweeping forces").

The third segment explains the various types of organizational
controls, including a section on "Quality Control." It begins: "A company which does not base its operations on quality is a company which
has no pride in its product. And further, it is generally to be expected
that a company which cannot control its quality cannot keep in control any of its other functions and activities. In other words, the state
of the quality of a company's products is a direct measure of the effectiveness of that company's management and operations." This statement had particular relevance, considering Japan's reputation as a
manufacturer of poor-quality goods for export. Cheap toys and trin-
kets, stamped with smeary ink *Made in Japan,* had created, for at least
two generations of Americans, an impression of Japan as an industrial
laughingstock.

In defining quality, the CCS authors drew on the writings of
Shewhart and Juran, and others. They included Juran's two definitions
of quality (quality of conformance, quality of design) as well as some
of his discussion about the cost of quality. They reproduced a chart re-
lating to the economics of the quality of design and identical in every
respect, except one label, to a chart printed in the first edition of Juran's
Handbook. Although they do not credit Juran (or any other sources) in
their 1949 typescript, much of Juran's material in the 1951 *Handbook*
had appeared earlier in papers and presentations; the definitions and
cost of quality discussion, for example, were featured in a paper presented to the Eighth International Management Congress in Stockholm Sweden, in 1947. According to Kenneth Hopper, the course
manual from 1950 cites L. P. Alford, a close colleague of Juran at

NYU, as a source. So, it is fair to say that some of Juran's key ideas—if not Juran himself—arrived in Japan even before Deming did.

The CCS courses made their mark on the communications managers; for some it was the first time they had heard of statistical quality control. Hopper wrote, "There can be little doubt that the Civil Communications Section and its engineers made an important contribution to Japanese industry and the Japanese economy" and he gathered much evidence to support that claim. "One of Japan's most famous companies," he revealed, "wrote Polkinghorn in 1950 telling him that his work would be 'immortal.' " Other testimony from participants is less adulatory. Hiroshi Toyoda says, "It was not that we were not doing any of these things before, but it was good to get it all into a structured form." Toshio Takahashi (then senior director of Kikuna Electric Company) gave the seminar more credit: "When we applied what we had learned at the seminar, we realized that what we had been doing was all wrong, and we were able to make dramatic progress."

For all of the CCS seminars usefulness, their impact had to be limited by a number of factors. Despite the considerable knowledge and experience of the three teachers, none of them was a recognized authority in business management or in quality control, either in Japan or in the United States. The text that supported them was not a published work; rather, it was a cut-and-paste job, a synthesis of many people's ideas and methods, cobbled together with occasional lapses of clarity, a typewritten volume filled with typos and illustrated with rudimentary diagrams. What's more, one of the seminar leaders (Sarasohn) was just thirty-three years old, an engineer with no experience as a senior manager in a large company. And, finally, the audience had been virtually coerced into attending. Sarasohn admits, "Everyone should have the experience of being a dictator once in his life." Their seminars, in other words, however well-intentioned they may have been, were—as David Halberstam describes later American lecturers—"however unconsciously, an exercise in power." So, although the course became institutionalized in Japan and was conducted for years

after the Occupation, it is not surprising that the names Magil, Sarasohn, Protzman, and Polkinghorn are not as well known or as revered
as Deming, Drucker, and Juran.

Sarasohn and Protzman had intended to create a second phase of
the course, designed for second-level managers and providing more
detail and specific information. But their plans were interrupted by the
invasion on June 25, 1950, of North Korean forces, in conjunction
with Chinese units, into South Korea, some seven hundred miles to
the west of Tokyo. On June 30, President Truman committed U.S.
troops to the conflict, and, a week later, appointed MacArthur as
Supreme Commander. "All of a sudden all hell broke loose in SCAP,"
recalls Sarasohn, "and so everything stopped." Now they would be
focused on Korea and Chinese communists, and would have no time
to develop the second phase of the *Industrial Management* course. Not
wanting to lose the momentum they had created, however, Sarasohn
says he "put in a call to Shewhart to have him come over and carry
on for us." Shewhart, however, was ill and could not travel. And so,
according to Sarasohn, the staffers at CCS cast about for a suitable re-
placement, preferably a disciple of Shewhart, and "there was this fellow at Columbia University by the name of Deming." Sarasohn knew
of Deming's work with the War Production Board—the "great job"
he had done—and put in a call to him via radio. But Sarasohn was not
the only one who suggested Deming.

THE ROLE OF JUSE

A small group of Japanese engineers and scientists had come together
informally during the war, to help with the war effort. They continued meeting after the war, to support the rebuilding of Japanese industry. They had no name, no formal positions; they were just a
handful of men who got together to drink *sake,* eat rice, and talk about
what to do. The food and drink, very scarce in Japan in those days,

came courtesy of one of the group's members, Dr. Nishiboro. He worked for Toshiba, in their electric bulb manufacturing operation. Light bulbs were as scarce as sake in postwar Japan, perhaps even more so. According to Deming's diary, "Dr. Nishiboro would fill his pockets with lamps, ride his bicycle out in the country, come back minus the light bulbs but with rice and *sake*."

Largely through the efforts of an engineer named Ken-ichi Koyanagi, the little group of about a dozen men endured. They took a formal title, the Japanese Union of Scientists and Engineers (JUSE). Although not actually a union, they used the term because SCAP had to approve all newly forming Japanese organizations, and MacArthur had made it known that unions were acceptable. There may also have been a political motive, as well. "JUSE clearly had a politicized heritage and an activist edge," writes William M. Tsutsui. "The inaugural issue of the organization's newsletter was headed with the slogan, 'Scientists and Engineers! Join hands for the sake of our native land!' and called for a 'united front in science and technology.'"

Koyanagi persuaded Ichiro Ishikawa to become associated with the group, and, eventually he agreed to take the title of chairman. This was an important association: Ishikawa was an influential figure in Japan—a member of a wealthy family, a respected professor, and first chairman of Keidanren, the Japan Federation of Economic Organizations, the most respected of Japan's business associations, which SCAP had recently allowed to return to activity.

"From the start, JUSE was keenly aware of its members' potential importance to Japan's economic recovery," writes William Tsutsui. "As managing director Koyanagi Ken-ichi observed in 1948, Japanese industry lacked many essential inputs—capital, raw materials, and so forth—but what it needed most desperately was modern scientific knowledge." In 1948, six members of JUSE formed a team to gain that knowledge by studying technology development in the United States and other Western countries; they called themselves the Quality Control Research Group. They began to gather material—writings by statisticians, engineers, and business administrators in the

United States and other Western countries. CCS provided them with some books on statistical quality control methods, including *Economic Control of Quality of Manufactured Product* by Walter Shewhart. They read E. S. Pearson, Harold F. Dodge, H. G. Romig, and translations of the American war standards. The team put together a seminar to present to their membership what they had learned about statistical quality control from these translated texts. The seminar, called *Statistical Analysis of Small Sample,* ran for the first time in September 1949, with Dr. Motosambure Masuyama as tutor. Thirty-nine engineers from seventeen corporations attended.

The course, while useful, made its organizers realize that, although the mathematical basis of statistics might apply without alteration in any culture, "in the case of quality control, or in anything that has the term 'control' attached to it, human and social factors are strongly at work," according to Kaoru Ishikawa, a member of that early team, and son of Chairman Ichiro Ishikawa. They decided they needed to know more; most important, they needed to adapt the body of knowledge about quality to Japanese culture and Japanese industry.

In December 1949, as they were struggling with their imperfect seminar, one of the JUSE members, Dr. Sigeiti Moriguti of Tokyo University, received a letter from Dr. Deming—whom they had read about in their research, and who some of them had met during his visit in 1947—which said that he would be visiting Japan in the spring of the following year. Koyanagi "thought that a course by a famous statistician like Dr. Deming could bring about epochal results." Somewhere along the line, JUSE also asked SCAP whom they might recommend as a speaker. A member of the staff in the Economic Science Section (ESS), Margaret Stone, had accompanied Deming on some of his travels in 1947 and remembered him as an expert on statistical quality control. She thought he might be a good choice.

So, with Deming being mentioned in so many quarters, the JUSE members decided he was the man to approach, but they did so in an oblique fashion. Koyanagi wrote a letter to Deming in March 1950, asking him to contribute a "message" to their new monthly magazine, *Statistical Quality Control.* The letter also inquired as to the exact date of Deming's arrival in Japan. Deming replied on March 22, saying he would visit in the summer. He asked for more details about the requested article and provided a list of people to whom JUSE should send their new magazine. (The list included thirteen names, including Shewhart, but not Juran.) Koyanagi recounts that, "Deeply moved by the kind letter, on 1 April we wrote again to Dr. Deming, informing him of the title and content of the article which we would like to have. In the same letter, we also asked if he could give a series of lectures on statistical quality control for several days while he was in Tokyo." Deming responded in April, saying he was "deeply honored" to be invited and suggested that the proposed seven-day seminar might be extended to eight days. "As for remuneration," he wrote, "I shall not desire any. It will be only a great pleasure to assist you." Deming, who was not a wealthy man, was able to make this generous offer because he would be receiving remuneration from SCAP for his work with the census.

Once Deming had agreed to conduct the course, Ichiro Ishikawa contacted the senior executives of the 200 companies with membership in JUSE at that time, asking them to send their engineers to attend. As the date grew closer—the first seminar was to be July 10—Ishikawa called them on the telephone to remind them and sent telegrams. He was serious and persuasive and, as chairman of the most important industrial organization in Japan, Keidanren, he was not a man to be lightly refused. "In 1950, refusing an invitation from Ishikawa was about as sensible as refusing a request from Don Corleone," writes Jerry Bowles, editor of *The Quality Executive*.

DEMING RETURNS

Deming was not a stranger to Japan when he arrived in 1950. He had first visited in January through March of 1947, as a member of a SCAP economic survey mission headed by Dr. A. S. Rice of Stanford University. As an expert in sampling methods, Deming's role was to help the Japanese develop a national census planned for 1951, and also

to consult with Japanese statisticians and American authorities on issues related to agriculture, housing, and Japanese fisheries.

Deming's stop in Japan was part of a tour around the world. He
had been in Greece to observe the elections, in March 1946, returned
there in the fall, then in November went on to India to consult with
government officials regarding sampling techniques. In January 1947,
Deming flew from Calcutta to Iwakuni, Japan. During his visit, he
traveled widely throughout the still-devastated land and made friends
with statisticians and economists, both American and Japanese. The
country and the people made a deep impression on him.

Three years later, in 1950, Deming was operating as a Consultant
in Statistical Studies and teaching statistics at the Graduate School of
Business at NYU. His published articles during the late 1940s show a
preoccupation with sampling and statistical methods applied to problems faced by governments. His book *Some Theory of Sampling* appeared in 1950. Deming, in short, was not primarily discoursing on
business management issues, or the management of quality, or even industrial quality control.

But the statistical methods that he cared so much about—and the
methods that had been so critical to War-time production (developed
primarily by Shewhart, popularized by Deming, promulgated by the
War Production Board, codified in military standards, institutionalized by the ASQC)—had dropped out of favor in the post-war years.
And so, Deming found himself more in demand as an expert in census taking and sampling techniques outside the United States (Greece,
India, Mexico, and Germany) than at home. When the invitation
came to visit Japan, Deming "bit at the lure" according to Sarasohn,
"precisely because he had been so discouraged after the war. He had
tried to talk to industry people and they wouldn't listen to him. And
then all the work he had done seemed to be going down the drain and
that made him very unhappy."

When Deming arrived in Japan on June 16, 1950, he came with the
pleasing knowledge that the Japanese considered him a world-class authority on statistical quality control for industry, and he was determined

to make the most of his 68-day visit. Starting July 10, he conducted two eight-day courses, in English, always with a Japanese interpreter: the first in Tokyo, with an attendance of 230 people and the second in Fukuoka (a city some 600 kilometers southwest of Tokyo, in the Kyushu region of Japan), with an attendance of 110. In addition to these eight-day courses, Deming delivered ten public lectures, to audiences as large as 600 people. In the afternoons, when he had time, he visited businesses and their manufacturing facilities. The evenings generally were devoted to dinner engagements and entertainments.

The Cycle: A Powerful Idea

Deming began his lectures to the engineers with a broad discussion of what he called a "new industrial age, created largely by statistical methods, principles and techniques." He argued that international trade was essential to peace and prosperity in Japan, and that it could only be conducted by attending to quality. He talked about the "chain of production" that included suppliers, employees within the manufacturing company, and—very important—customers. (Later, Deming would say that he taught the Japanese that manufacturing is a system, probably referring to his comments about the production chain.) "'Good quality' and 'uniform quality' have no meaning except with reference to the consumer's needs," Deming continued, and explained that, in order to establish reliable and economical communication with the consumer, "it is necessary to carry out statistical tests and surveys." And, in this way, Deming's love and understanding of sampling, particularly of populations of people, intersect with his ideas about quality. Statistical methods, for Deming, were not reserved for understanding the production line, they also provided a valuable tool for understanding the customer.

Deming concluded his introductory remarks with a discussion of the manufacturing process as a whole. Manufacturing had long

Figure 5.2   The Old Way according to Deming.

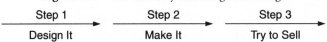

been conducted, said Deming, in three independent steps, shown in Figure 5.2.

Deming's simple chart was based on a drawing contained in Shewhart's *Statistical Method from the Viewpoint of Quality Control*, published in 1939 by the Graduate School of the Department of Agriculture. Deming had brought Shewhart to the Department to conduct a series of lectures, which were gathered into this book, for which Deming wrote an introduction. (This was one of the books the JUSE Quality Control Research Group had read.) Shewhart's version of the Old Way of manufacturing, shown in Figure 5.3, also consisted of three steps, which, he said, correspond to the three steps in a dynamic scientific process of acquiring knowledge: hypothesis, experiment, test.

The difference between the two depictions of manufacturing is that Deming broadened the scope. For Shewhart's "Specification," which implies the defining of measures and tolerances, Deming substituted the larger "Design It," which implies the entire new-product-development process. Shewhart's "Production" is equivalent to Deming's more demotic "Make It." But the most important difference is Deming's change of "Inspection" to "Try to Sell," which extends the manufacturing activity well beyond the end of the production line ("Inspection") and out into the world of the customer (selling).

Deming then went on to describe the New Way, which is represented in Figure 5.4.

Figure 5.3   The Old Way according to Shewhart. (Reprinted by permission from W. A. Shewhart, *Statistical Method from the Viewpoint of Quality Control,* edited by W. E. Deming, 1939. Washington, DC: Graduate School of the Department of Agriculture. Reprinted 1986 by Dover Publications, New York.)

Step 1	Step 2	Step 3
Specification	Production	Inspection

Figure 5.4 The New Way according to Deming.

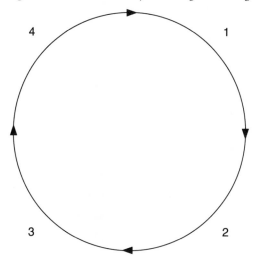

"In the new way, management introduces, through consumer research, a fourth step," said Deming, "and runs through the four steps in a *cycle,* over and over."

1. Design the product (with appropriate tests).
2. Make it, test it, in the production line and in the laboratory.
3. Put it on the market.
4. Test it in service, through market research, find out what the user thinks of it, and why the nonuser has not bought it.

To the four steps, Deming then adds a fifth: Redesign the product. And so the steps become a continuously repeating process. Deming's New Way was also based on a Shewhart cycle, which contained only three steps, arrayed in a circle, as shown in Figure 5.5.

Deming further recommended that manufacturing and marketing should begin "on a pilot scale" and then be built up, "as fast as market conditions indicate" through repetition of the four-step cycle. To

Figure 5.5   The New Way according to Shewhart. (Reprinted by permission from
W. A. Shewhart, *Statistical Method from the Viewpoint of Quality Control,* edited by W. E.
Deming, 1939. Washington, DC: Graduate School of the Department of Agriculture.
Reprinted 1986 by Dover Publications, New York.)

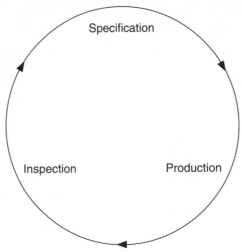

depict that repetition of the cycle, Deming suggested a spiral, as shown
in Figure 5.6.

After these opening remarks, Deming then went into a fairly
straightforward explication of the main ideas and tools involved in
quality control: variation, control charts, and acceptance sampling.

Deming's cycle was particularly attractive to the Japanese. It implied that they could improve their manufacturing operations in small
steps. They did not have to invest huge amounts of capital, which were
not available, to radically change their processes or install expensive
new machinery. They didn't have to create great factories like the
ones they had seen or heard about in the United States—the Haw-
thornes and River Rouges and Schenectady Works. (Eiji Toyoda, for
example, would come to the conclusion that mass production, of the
type he had studied at Ford's plants, "could never work in Japan.")
Rather, they could improve through the application of human resources—brains and willpower—which they had in far greater abundance than resources of money, machinery, or raw materials. This was

Figure 5.6 The manufacturing cycle in repetition according to Deming.

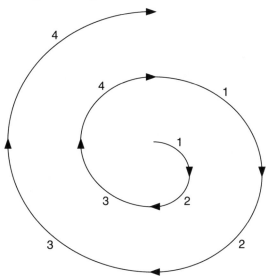

a very simple and powerful idea. Yes, Sarasohn and Protzman had explained how American companies organized and how they inspected their work, but those were methods and practices. Here was an *idea* the Japanese could understand and could make their own.

The Japanese have a genius for importing powerful ideas from other cultures, adapting them to their own needs, interpreting them in their own ways, and applying them with peculiar consistency and vigor. "The Japanese people are very good at modification of this kind," explains Hajime Karatsu, professor at Tokyo University. "The characters we use in the Japanese language were originally imported from China. Likewise, we imported very complicated statistical methods from the United States and modified them." In fact, the teachings of Deming and, later, Juran, were not the first ideas about business management to be imported from America by the Japanese. Frederick Taylor's *Principles of Scientific Management* was translated into Japanese, with the title, *The Secret of Saving Lost Motion,* soon after its publication in 1911, and is reported to have sold 1.5 million copies.

Disturbing Déjà Vu

Despite the outpouring of interest in his lectures, Deming had a bad moment during the very first day of his first eight-day course, a depressing feeling of déjà vu. He looked out at the faces in the audience and saw a mass of highly attentive students—"I've never had better students," he wrote—but he had the sinking feeling that they were the wrong students. They were similar to the earnest engineers and scientists he had lectured to in the United States, during the war and after. Yes, they would listen to him and might implement his methods, but they would not have the authority or influence to affect the whole of the business enterprise. In other words, he imagined that what had happened in America might happen again in Japan: After an initial rush of interest in statistical methods, there would be a return to the same old ways of doing things.

"My duty became clear," wrote Deming later. "Top management, through Mr. Ishikawa, had invited me, and I must explain to them their obligations, responsibilities, and methods for improvement of quality. Quality begins at the top. It seemed to me that quality of product and of service can be no better than the intent of top management. The only way Japan could experience success would be for top management to be committed to the course of action." And so, Deming met with Ishikawa and explained to him the importance of getting the message to senior management. It took three meetings, but Ishikawa finally took the point. He sent off a telegram to twenty-one of Japan's most important senior executives, inviting them to dinner with Dr. Deming on Tuesday, July 13. Jerry Bowles provides an intriguing analysis of Ishikawa's motives:

> It is unlikely, however, that Ishikawa wanted the business leaders there to be introduced to the concept of statistical quality control, for the simple reason that statistical methods had been introduced four years earlier and were already being widely promoted in industry.

A more likely reason for Ichiro Ishikawa's Deming dinner is that he wanted Japan's new industrial leaders to hear, from this tall [Deming stood 6'1"], loud, terrifying gaijin—a slightly derogatory word used to connote anyone who isn't Japanese—what has been Deming's central message for the past 60 years: that they—management—were the problem, and that nothing would get better until they took personal responsibility for change.

All the invited executives showed up at the Industry Club at 5:00 P.M. on the appointed day. Deming spoke to them for about an hour. "There was a lot of wealth represented in that room," he writes, "and a lot of power." By the end of the evening, the executives were talking about meeting with Dr. Deming again, perhaps for a conference in a nice setting outside the city, maybe in the mountains west of Tokyo. That dinner meeting, claims Deming with typical grandeur, "was the birth of the new Japan."

Three days before Deming was to leave Japan, the conference took place. Forty-six executives joined Deming for two days and one night at a hot springs resort in the town of Hakone, 100 kilometers west of Tokyo. According to Jungi Noguchi, a longtime JUSE member, Deming talked about the importance of the practical application of statistical methods, and how quality control is the best method for producing—economically—what customers want. Deming's very presence—a "technical" authority sharing dinner at a fancy resort with Japan's top executives—was as significant as the details of what he said. The essence of his message to the executives might be boiled down to: Quality control is more than a discipline for your engineers, it is of vital importance to the success of your business. You should pay serious attention to it.

Deming left Japan having met with, by his own estimation, more than 1,000 engineers, managers, and scholars. Not only did his visit establish his own reputation in Japan, it helped get JUSE on its feet. According to Deming, JUSE had charged each of the 440 attendees 15,000 yen (about $42) for the course, for a total of nearly $18,000 (although Noguchi claims the registration fee was only 5,000 yen). In

addition, JUSE collected the notes from Deming's lectures and published them as a booklet entitled *Dr. W. Edwards Deming's Lectures on
Statistical Control of Quality, 1950, Tokyo,* which sold for about 400 yen
(about $1.12). The first printing sold about 2,000 copies; a second edi-
tion, with revisions by Deming and retitled *Elementary Principles of the
Statistical Control of Quality,* sold another 3,700 copies in two printings.
The royalties on sales of about $6,300 from the booklet "amounted to
a sizable amount"—approximately 300,000 yen, (around $700 by 1960)
according to Noguchi—"and Mr. Koyanagi naturally offered to pay
them" to Deming. But Deming declined the offer and instead donated
them to JUSE, to be used "for any conscientious purpose." Koyanagi
decided that the most conscientious use of the money would be to establish a quality prize, an idea that the JUSE board approved in December 1950. Deming's donated royalties served as a foundation for
the cash prize. The first Deming prizes were awarded in 1951.

Sarasohn left Japan at the end of 1950, having accomplished his
mission. He stayed four years longer than he had intended. "We got
radio production going," he recalls. David Halberstam corroborates
Sarasohn's claim: "The first two successful consumer appliances were
radios and sewing machines, both of them inexpensive. Television had
not yet arrived, and radio offered a form of larger community and
free entertainment." Upon his return to the United States, Sarasohn
joined the consulting firm Booz, Allen and Hamilton, in Chicago.
Later, he moved to New York to work for IBM, and retired as Corporate Director of Engineering in 1977.

IN SEARCH OF NEW INSPIRATION

Deming returned to Japan in 1951. "Expecting to be dazzled with
new statistical advances from abroad," writes Tsutsui, "many Japanese
observers were discouraged to find that Deming had no new tricks to
pull from his statistical hat." The application of statistical methods

had, in fact, not been entirely successful. Like the introduction of the control chart in the early days at Western Electric, some of the statistical techniques were too advanced for the state of Japanese postwar manufacturing. In addition, statistical methods were so narrowly focused on manufacturing that they had little effect on the broader problems of the Japanese business organization. "A growing concern of the JUSE leaders was that Japanese experts, by scrupulously following their American mentors, had become excessively theoretical in their conception of quality control. The general impression was that, fired by a precocious zeal to learn from the United States, Japanese students of QC had fixated on the statistical paraphernalia of quality control while ignoring the question of how to apply their textbook knowledge to actual workshop situations."

In 1952, Deming sent a copy of Juran's recently published *Quality Control Handbook* to JUSE, according to Eizo Watanabe, one of the members of the Quality Control Research Group. Later that year, Koyanagi traveled to the United States, and, at an ASQC meeting in Rochester, New York, Deming introduced him to Juran. Koyanagi had been impressed by the *Handbook* and thought Juran might be able to provide JUSE with the fresh perspective on quality that they sorely needed. Juran eagerly accepted, but, because of some scheduled minor surgery, he was unable to make the trip until two years later.

Juran arrived in Tokyo on July 4, 1954. Tokyo looked grim to him, despite the great strides that had been made since the city's near-complete devastation. He saw a city that consisted primarily of one- and two story buildings, its streets and the outlying roads crowded with overloaded bicycles and three-wheeled minitrucks. Japan had, however, come a long way from its low point at the end of the war. By June of 1950, when the North Koreans invaded South Korea, real wages had exceeded those of Japan's last boom period, 1934–1936. Industrial production then zoomed upward, much of it to serve the demand for war matériel required in the Korean War. By 1952, more than 60 percent of international receipts for all Japanese production came from goods consumed in the war. The American occupation ended in 1952, spurring further growth. People had greater purchasing power and a mass market began to emerge. In addition to the demand for radios and sewing machines, consumers now began to crave the "three electric treasures": a television, a washing machine, and a refrigerator. By 1955, the gross national product (GNP) returned to its pre-war level, and began growing at a phenomenal rate: it grew 10 percent faster each year than any other national economy, and three times faster than that of the United States. In addition, the *zaibatsu* had begun to knit themselves back together, so that senior management was stronger and deeper than it had been during the CCS course of 1949 and Deming's visit a year later.

But, despite the advances of the previous eight years, in the year of Juran's first visit, 1954, Japanese businesses still faced many problems—some new, some old. Professor Shigeto Tsuru, Director of the Economic Research Institute at Hitotsubashi University in Tokyo, painted a gloomy picture of Japan's prospects, in a 1955 article in *Atlantic Monthly:* "Japan's phenomenal postwar recovery might perhaps be more apparent than real." By the summer of 1954, when Juran arrived, "there was little left of the scaffolding erected to help build a new Japan." The ending of the Korean War, in July 1953, was a major factor in Japan's economic difficulties. The production of war matériel was, according to Tsuru, "precisely that category of goods to which Japan should have given little, if any, priority in the process of sound recovery." Businesses that had plunged into the production of war matériel now had to convert back to making other products. Japan still suffered a huge imbalance of trade, spending some $2.4 billion to buy food, raw materials, and other goods, and taking in only $1.3 billion from sale of exports. "Japan depends at present on other countries for 87 percent of essential industrial raw materials," continued Tsuru, "including coking coal, iron ore, crude oil, raw cotton, wool, crude rubber, zinc ore, industrial salt, phosphate rock, soya beans, bauxite, etc." In addition, Japan could only supply 80 percent of its own food. "In order to balance her trade," prescribed Tsuru, "Japan's exports will have to be increased by a minimum of 40 percent." Arthur H.

Dean, Deputy Secretary of State under President Eisenhower, agreed: "What Japan requires most of all over the long term is foreign markets in which she can sell at a reasonable profit the products of the export industry."

The business conditions that surrounded Juran's 1954 visit probably contributed to the great attention he received from Japan's most powerful senior executives. He began the visit with two lectures in Tokyo; with 70 people attending each two-day session, he addressed a total audience of 140. The group was composed primarily of CEOs from Japan's largest manufacturing companies—the kind of audience Deming had had to plead with Ishikawa to produce. This surprised Juran. "Never, before my 1954 trip to Japan," he recalled in 1993, "and never since, has the industrial leadership of a major power given me so much of its attention. Once in the United States, just a few months ago, I faced an audience of 70 leading CEOs, but that was for one hour." In addition to the CEOs, the audience had its share of academics, including Kaoru Ishikawa.

Juran proved to be something of a novelty for the Japanese. Juran's style was quiet and reserved, though still forceful and authoritative. He was an American citizen, but he had been born in Europe; he didn't look particularly American, and he didn't have the broadest of American mannerisms. He wasn't physically big. He didn't smoke, nor did he drink. And he came with his wife. Mrs. Juran was a calm, quiet, comfortable presence, with a warm smile and a down-to-earth approach. The Japanese industrialists found her unthreatening, compatible with their ideal of the proper wife (whether they personally idolized it or not) and unlike the American stereotype. Juran came to refer to his wife as Okusan, "the honorable person of the inner house." "That's the way Japanese wives are supposed to behave. And, of course, I've tended to be a fairly private person, so my main concern was with knowledge transfer."

The Japanese may have respected these traits in Juran more than they enjoyed them. Junji Noguchi remembers that Juran came across as a "strict professor. He doesn't drink. He doesn't smoke. Dr. Deming, on the other hand, likes to drink very much. And he also really enjoys going to drinking places, he likes parties and so forth. That's why the people in Japan consider Dr. Deming an easy person to get along with." Another early JUSE member agreed, only half-facetiously, that Dr. Juran "should drink more."

Juran scored one technological coup in his lectures. He worked with a startling device, seldom seen in Japan, the overhead projector. He used it with consummate skill, writing with a crisp authority, the letters well and swiftly formed. There can be something mesmerizing (and, in the wrong hands, paralyzing) about an overhead projector presentation. The presentation is often paced by the forming of words on acetate, and the audience is forced into a kind of intellectual suspense, watching as each new idea appears on the screen. Add to that the calming whir of the cooling fan, the squeaky counterpoint of the marker, the gentle half-dark required to see the image, and the mysterious lighting on the presenter's face as he or she peers down at his task. Juran's projector made such an impression on his audience that he left the machine behind as a gift to his hosts.

In addition to his lectures, Juran toured factories in Tokyo, including the makers of chemicals, steel, electrical equipment, and cameras. In those days, it was rare for a Japanese senior manager—or an American, for that matter—to venture onto the factory floor. But Juran insisted that the company president accompany him when he took a tour of a plant. "In those days, a Japanese president did not think that he himself should visit the manufacturing site. But Dr. Juran always made it a rule to accompany a company president when he visited the manufacturing site. There were a lot of surprising things to be found in the factories. In that way, Dr. Juran gave the Japanese presidents very good lessons."

And, on the tour—often wearing a hard hat—Juran listened to people, really *listened* to them. "Dr. Juran always lent ears to other people," remembers one of his executive students. "He really listened very carefully to what other people said, regardless of who it was.

Ordinarily speaking, when some person of authority says something, people would listen to him. But Juran's attitude was that, he would talk with and ask questions of workers in the plant. He was very receptive and accepting of other people's opinions." Juran never toured without his notepad and pencil. He jotted down facts and observations, tidbits of information that he would file away for later use. "He always had a little card in his pocket, and a pencil. When we discussed, he would write something. A short sentence, and tuck it in his pocket," recalls Professor Yoshio Kondo.

"Dr. Juran was like a magician to us," agrees Hajime Karatsu. "We would collect data from the shop floor and hand the data to Dr. Juran. He would analyze the data and produce a chart. He was very good at identifying problems. So, he seemed like a magician to us. And that was very inspiring."

The conditions Juran found in the Japanese factories also made a strong impression on him. "The work methods in the factories were inefficient due to lack of mechanization, automation, etc. This was understandable since at that time the supply of hand labor was plentiful and low-priced, whereas the supply of machinery was limited and costly. I was astounded to observe the work pace achieved by the workers in those old, unsafe plants. The pace was greater than I had seen in the West in plants operating under piecework incentive, and I wondered how this was possible. My hosts explained to me the implications of the Japanese concept of mutual lifelong responsibilities between worker and company."

Juran conducted a two-day seminar in Hakone for senior executives. Following that, he led a seminar for middle managers of industrial divisions or units. Then he traveled to Osaka, where he repeated the process, starting with factory visits and following up with seminars for another 140 CEOs and 300 middle managers who represented Japan's major manufacturers of textiles, paper, steel, chemicals, glass, pharmaceuticals, and electrical equipment. The Jurans flew home on August 17, 1954.

JURAN'S MESSAGE

Juran's lectures to the Japanese were well-organized and precise. Much of the material was based on the *Quality Control Handbook* and so, in the writing, had been carefully thought through; the ideas were well supported by case examples and reference articles. Juran defined his terms precisely and employed them consistently.

His principal message, or at least the message that was principally heard, according to some who attended, was that quality was as much about management as it was about statistics and control charts, cycles and surveys. He began his first lecture this way:

> In presenting these lectures, I am conscious that there are great differences in customs between countries. These differences sometimes make it unwise for one to generalize unless there is a clear understanding of the customs of the countries involved.
>
> Naturally, where we are dealing with the basic laws of nature, there are no differences between countries. The laws of gravitation and of thermodynamics apply with equal force in Japan and in the United States.
>
> However, in the field of management (and much of what we are going to be discussing does lie in the field of management), we are dealing, to a large degree, in human relations. These human relations are very strongly influenced by the customs prevailing in the various countries.

He went on to say that the "ingredients in the economic formula" are not equally available in different countries. "For example, in the United States, where capital is plentiful and wages are high, we find companies willing to undertake large expenditures for mechanization and other labor saving methods. In other countries, the relationships between cost of capital and cost of wages are different, and these differences strongly influence the final decisions made." Juran thus acknowledged, if obliquely, the need for Japan to improve through methods other than the capital-intensive, technology-based solutions so beloved by manufacturers in the United States.

Juran then methodically discussed his fundamental ideas. They included his bifurcated definition of quality (of design and of conformance), the economics of quality, and the never-ending cycle of improvement—a strategy for creating improvements, little by little, one by one, that gradually accrete into big changes and huge improvements over time. This cycle, which was detailed in the *Handbook,* was called the "atom." (See Figure 5.7.) The atom, which has similarities to both Shewhart's and Deming's cycles, defined an "unvarying sequence of activity" that determined "any quality characteristic."

In the first edition of the *Handbook,* Juran applied the idea of the quality atom quite narrowly to characteristics of quality. In later editions, and other writings, Juran broadened the atom until it became a spiral, similar to Deming's, and identified the unvarying sequence of activities involved in improving quality throughout an organization—from market research to use and customer feedback. In 1954, Juran had yet to fully develop his "universal sequence" of steps to be followed to

Figure 5.7 The quality atom. (From J. M. Juran, *Quality Control Handbook* (1st ed.), 1951. New York: McGraw-Hill. Reproduced with permission of McGraw-Hill Companies.)

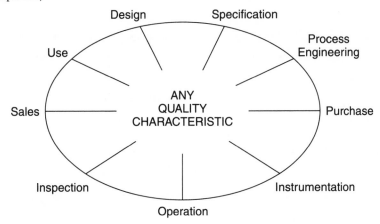

accomplish what he came to call "breakthrough" improvement, but he did offer an early description of the steps involved in achieving quality control:

1. Selection of control points.
2. Definition of units of measure.
3. A systematic means for measuring and summarizing actual performance.
4. Selection of standards of performance.
5. Interpretation of the difference between actual performance and standard.
6. Decision on what action to take.
7. Action to comply with that decision.

Juran asserted that these steps can be applied to any business process, including order processing, accounting, and production.

MANAGEMENT INVOLVEMENT

Juran's most important, and lasting message to the Japanese came in a special lecture, delivered only to top executives. "The Japanese didn't have to buy me a plane ticket to learn about quality inspections," writes Juran. "That was in the book." The Japanese "did get their money's worth" however, with his thoughts on how managers should take charge of quality and what their role should be. He identified the responsibilities relative to the quality function that must belong to management:

1. Responsibility for high policy or doctrine.
2. Responsibility for choice of quality of design (grade).
3. Responsibility for the plan of organization of the company with respect to quality.

4. Responsibility for setting up measurement of what is actually taking place with respect to quality.

5. Responsibility for reviewing results against goals and for taking action on significant variations.

Deming had argued the case for quality control to many of Japan's senior executives during the Hakone session, and it seems that his audience came to believe in the importance of quality to their operations. "Prior to Dr. Deming's visit, Japanese quality control had been butting against a wall created by adherence to difficult statistics theories. This wall, however, was torn down through Dr. Deming's eight-day courses," writes Noguchi.

Juran helped the Japanese to break through another wall, one that separated senior managers from the implementation of quality methods. Juran told them that they personally had to take responsibility for quality; they had to get involved in setting quality policy, in developing products, in organizing for quality, and in making sure that quality was actually being achieved. This is quite different from saying, as Deming seems to have said, that the senior executive should recognize the role of quality and support the quality efforts of staff members. Juran told them what they needed to do, and how to go about doing it. As Tsutsui puts it: "Juran's inspiration was like a 'welcome rain' to JUSE's parched and wilting quality crusade."

He recommended that everyone in the company should receive training in quality, including top executives and department heads. Although many top executives sat in Juran's audience, it is one thing for a senior manager to attend a lecture by a visiting world-famous authority like Deming or Juran, quite another to sit through a one-day training course conducted by a lower-level staff member. Juran cautioned his audience of middle managers that much preparatory work should be applied to presenting the case for quality to senior executives. "There should be a presentation of the essential facts as to the company's quality, its competitive position, the relation with customers, the strengths and the deficiencies of the existing plan of quality control." Juran, no doubt remembering his own difficulties in breaching the walls of the executive suites at Western Electric, still speaks with particular care about this issue.

What's more, Juran said, not only must quality be the concern of management, executives must in turn make quality the concern of *everyone* in the organization: the secretary, the finance person, the maintenance worker, the salesperson, the cook, the purchaser, the marketer. He further discussed the relationships among the various disciplines and activities within an organization, including production, technology, testing, accounting, sales, marketing, materials management, human resources, and the rest. Juran sums up his message to the Japanese by saying that he talked "about the organizational barriers to quality management and I suggested that they try to find ways to institutionalize programs within their companies that would yield continuous quality improvement. That is exactly what they did. And around those programs the Japanese built a quality revolution."

These messages certainly resounded in the ears of the middle managers and engineers in the audience. One JUSE member, Masumasa Imaizumi, professor at Musashi Institute in Tokyo, remembers: "Top management people were concerned with increasing market share, and gaining more profit. That was what filled their minds in those days. They didn't talk with us about quality." Takashi Ken Kayano agrees: "Japanese management people didn't lend their ears to you. But when a person like Dr. Juran says the same thing, they are always willing to listen. I think this is more true of Japanese nature than of some others. A foreign expert of a certain field would be very much listened to very carefully by Japanese management. Even if the foreign expert is not really an expert, Japanese people will listen to them more than a fellow Japanese expert."

Today, the call for management involvement in quality sounds obvious. Even in 1954, the message already had been delivered to the Japanese by Magil, Protzman, and Sarasohn. Deming had said essentially the same thing: *Management must take charge of quality!* He had said that quality should be their top priority, and that quality came even before profit.

Juran delivered the message perhaps more succinctly and persuasively than those who came before him. He also delivered it at a time when it was ready to be heard and acted on.

Imaizumi remembers: "In 1954, when Dr. Juran came to Japan, nobody expected that the quality revolution would take place in the future. Quality was so bad in those days, the customers were always complaining about the quality of our products. I was in charge of quality then, so I always had to apologize to the customers all the time and I was really worried. Dr. Juran taught us a way to look at things from a different perspective that we were totally unaware of: quality. Dr. Juran would not give us instructions as to what we should do. He would tell us: you should think as to what we should do and really think hard." Noguchi concurs: "Dr. Deming taught us statistical quality control, but today's total quality control, participated by all employees of an organization, is based on Dr. Juran's lessons." Adds Yoshiano Nakada of Bell Labs, "He taught that quality can be planned and about customer focus." Deming wrote that Juran's "masterful teaching gave to Japanese management new insight into management's responsibility for improvement of quality and productivity."

But, as Juran writes, the "unsung heroes of the Japanese quality revolution were the Japanese managers." Noguchi agrees: "We don't have a special method. The quality control activity in Japan is nothing but cooperation and harmony of the people. The cooperation of the people working at the same work place is the basis for everything."

It is intriguing to note that, in 1969, JUSE proposed the establishment of a Juran prize, to be awarded to companies that had won the Deming prize several times. Unprepared for the offer, Juran balked; the Japanese interpreted his hesitation as a refusal. JUSE member Ichiro Miyauchi expresses regret that they did not introduce a Juran award (although it was established as the Japan prize). "It was because of his sincerity and honesty that Dr. Juran refused to introduce this award. We listened to his view, but I think we were wrong. If we had introduced the Juran award, I'm sure that the world would have recognized his importance."

6

Breakthrough and Bliss

(1954–1975)

The remainder of the journey promises to be a storybook voyage.

J. M. Juran

⚜

THE FREELANCE LIFE

J uran's invitation to Japan was only one indication of the new status he attained with the publication of the *Handbook*. Not only did it garner him invitations to Japan and other countries, as well as speaking engagements and consulting assignments, it provided the basis for a long period of what he calls "blissful freelancing." The success of the book not only changed his life, it changed his attitude. In 1955, he wrote of his pre-*Handbook* life as "a careening journey, in a fog of fear, fueled by intense determination. Periodically, I foundered on this rock and that, only to collect my wits and dash off into another direction. Big sail and small rudder. But now, the fog has magically lifted. There is still much sail, but the rudder has grown to a more appropriate size. The remainder of the journey promises to be a storybook voyage, the ship on course, a good wind, and a firm hand at the helm."

During this voyage of nearly three decades (1951–1979), Juran adhered to the model he had created with an intense, unrelenting— sometimes obsessive, sometimes abrasive—application of energy. Juran published regularly: a steady stream of books (16, translated into at least a dozen languages), hundreds of articles in a variety of journals, a library of videotapes and workbooks. He spoke at meetings and forums and conventions. He conducted hundreds of seminars and training courses, many in conjunction with the American Management Association. He took on a myriad of consulting assignments, which took him into companies and organizations throughout the United States and in forty countries around the world.

As each activity fed into the others, Juran could play many roles in the worldwide business community. He could be an investigator and a researcher, learning from his clients and students what they were doing in the field—gathering information, data, ideas, methods. He could be a synthesizer, by analyzing his field-gathered information, shaping it, and articulating it in his speaking and writing. He could be an observer and analyst on world events, interpreting for his audiences what was happening and what he believed to be important. He could be an advocate and proponent for quality, using his knowledge and ubiquity to influence everything from individual companies to professional societies to government policy.

The unifying factor in all this activity was the virtually continuous revision and regular republication of the *Quality Control Handbook*. First published in 1951, subsequent editions appeared in 1962, 1974, and 1988. The fourth edition had grown to an encyclopedic 1,800 pages. Juran organized himself around the *Handbook,* meticulously gathering information—on the pad or notebook or scrap of paper he always carried with him—and filing it in the appropriate chapter folder. Associates, clients, and acquaintances throughout the world had noted this characteristic Juran habit. In the factory, the boardroom, or the seminar room, Juran would notice some intriguing practice or technique. Out would come the notebook and pencil, and a careful notation would be made. Or, when a seminar attendee would make an interesting point, Juran would instantly jot it down and tuck it in his pocket and thus into his mind. Any request made of him was similarly jotted down, and invariably answered, in time.

The model was so successful and satisfying that, by 1966, Juran indulged himself to write about the consulting business itself. He describes the rigors of consultancy, including an abundance of travel (75,000–100,000 air miles annually, he calculates), many nights away from home, and many "short weekends," and he reveals the healthy fees charged by management consultants in that era: between $100 and $300 per day. But, to Juran, the peripatetic lifestyle and substantial financial rewards were not the major attractions of the consulting profession. "With broader experience, mounting prestige and growth in earned authority," Juran writes, "a freedom is achieved which is exhilarating beyond description. The problem of income has been solved so that the consultant can be quite selective in his engagements. His writings have disseminated his experience and ideas nationally and internationally. The invitations to lecture, to write, to provide services, are increasingly interesting and flattering. With his newfound freedom, he need not bargain closely. He can take on challenging assignments even if they involve only a nominal fee, or no fee at all. Yet in dealing with well-heeled people, his proposals for a full fee are not debated. And he reaches a state of considerable latitude in scheduling his time. If he receives an invitation to lecture abroad, there is no need to ask the bureaucracy if he may go. He just goes." For a man who began working at the age of nine, labored in an obdurate bureaucracy for seventeen years, and scrambled for six years to put together an independent career, the ultimate reward was freedom.

THE UNIVERSAL SEQUENCES

Over the years, Juran continued to refine his ideas about the process of achieving quality, and how it can best be managed. In *Management of Inspection and Quality Control* (1945), Juran had argued that upper management should have quality-mindedness—an idea he presented later to his audiences in Japan:

> In the absence of sincere manifestations of interest at the top, little will happen below. Intermediate executives properly occupy themselves with those problems which appear to interest top management. The interest of top management usually stems from the desire to achieve a good quality reputation among the consuming public. It is generally realized by top management that such a reputation is clearly a valuable asset. What is too frequently not realized is that the achievement of such a quality reputation requires that the idea—the propaganda—permeate the entire organization.

He then discussed the steps involved in the successful implementation of a quality control program, but did so within the environment of the "shop" and its inspectors and engineers. In 1964, however, Juran had gathered enough information and had crystallized his ideas sufficiently to articulate two "universal sequences" for the management of quality. He published them in *Managerial Breakthrough*. The first sequence is for achieving *breakthrough* in quality, the second is for achieving *control* of quality. Juran "pleads innocent of invention" in both these sequences. They are, he says, universal sequences of actions "invented or reinvented" by managers in many situations and only "restated in a more generalized, orderly form" by him.

"All managerial activity is directed at either Breakthrough or Control," Juran writes. "Managers are busy doing both of these things, and nothing else." Control, he says, "means staying on course, adherence to standard, prevention of change. Under complete control, nothing would change—we would be in a static, quiescent world. This isn't as bad as it sounds. For a good many things, it would be wonderful to have no change." Meeting sales quotas, achieving specifications, staying within budget, meeting delivery schedules—lack of change in such activities can be positive. This idea of managerial control has its roots in manufacturing control and Shewhart's control chart: A process or activity that is under control is one that is not affected by special, unwanted, variation. It is stable, reliable, and consistent. But, of course, it is still affected by random variation—the fluctuations and changes that are considered to be inherent to any system.

Breakthrough, by contrast, "means change, a dynamic, decisive movement to new higher levels of performance. In a truly static society, breakthrough is taboo, forbidden." But static societies will always be threatened by a variety of basic human drives; people will always want more than they now have, more knowledge, more goods, more power. So, static societies generally become extinct, argues Juran, as do biological species that fail to adapt and improve.

> Biologists estimate that of the species that have lived at one time or other on this earth, over 98 percent are now extinct. There is no corresponding estimate as to the rate of extinction of industrial companies, products, processes, organization forms, procedures, etc. However, the mortality rate has been high and seems to be picking up in tempo.

The significance of this rate of extinction is that, as with living organisms, the products, processes, methods, etc., of industry, are only mortal. They are doomed from birth. If the company is to outlive them, it must provide for a birth rate in excess of the death rate.

It is this basic urge to outlive its mortal components which drives the company, through its managers, to find new products, processes, markets; to reduce costs, accidents, absences; to increase output, quality, profits. Only through such "good" changes can the company stay alive, strong, fresh. Failing in this, the company ages, decays, and dies.

This statement of the need for breakthrough change—in products, processes, attitudes, markets—applies as well to today's business conditions as to those of the mid-1960s. But, says Juran, both breakthrough and control are necessary for the survival and health of a company. Breakthrough brings good changes; control prevents bad ones.

In his early work, Juran had begun wrestling with the idea of a universal sequence for achieving quality. "I'd been brooding over that for a long time," he says. But, at the time of his Japanese lectures, "The idea that you could find a sequence of steps that would fit any program, that hadn't dawned on me at that time. That took the experience of a number of examples."

The breakthrough sequence is based on scientific method, which has, of course, evolved over the centuries: gather data, formulate a hypothesis, test the hypothesis through experiment, then accept, modify, or discard the hypothesis based on analysis of the tests. The Shewhart/Deming cycle (as discussed on page 115) was based on this scientific method, and became institutionalized and popularized in a variety of forms:

PDCA	Plan, Do, Check, Act
PDCA	Plan, Do, Check, Action
PDSA	Plan, Do, Study, Act
EPDCA	Evaluate, Plan, Do, Check, Amend

But these cycles or sequences of steps do not distinguish between control and breakthrough, as Juran's sequences do. Juran also provides a great deal of detail about how to organize for breakthrough or control, along with discussion about the issues that arise along the way. In subsequent writings and, later, in a series of videotapes, Juran continued to refine the steps of the breakthrough sequence into the following topics.

Breakthrough in Attitudes

A determination to make a breakthrough change will always come, says Juran, from an individual with an idea. "Any individual, any idea. An operator drops a grimy form into the suggestion box. A vice president brings a magazine article to a staff meeting. A district manager gets a tip from a customer. A staff specialist is set afire by a speech he hears at a conference. A supervisor vows 'We'll fix this thing once and for all.'" Although breakthrough may *originate* with anyone, from anywhere in the company, that does not mean that breakthrough can be *achieved* from the bottom up. The determination and commitment to make a change must always come from one or more senior managers.

And, although an idea for breakthrough often comes from the middle layers of a company, that breakthrough attitude is more likely to erupt in a company in which senior managers have already created a climate that encourages breakthrough thinking, and in which an organized approach to breakthrough exists and is supported.

The Pareto Principle

Once an objective of change has been determined, the next step in Juran's sequence is to settle on a project that will help accomplish the objective. This step serves to narrow down the possible options for achieving the goal to one clearly defined course of action, usually involving a project that can be managed and is measurable.

One method for determining which project to pursue is Pareto Analysis. Juran had first been exposed to Pareto's ideas in the 1930s, during a visit to General Motors. He used the term in the first edition of the *Quality Control Handbook,* in a caption to a graph showing the Maldistribution of Quality Losses. In a 1954 article, he talked of the Pareto Curve.

In all its iterations, the basic idea remained the same. "In any series of elements to be controlled," writes Juran, "a selected small fraction, in terms of number of elements, always accounts for a large fraction, in terms of effect." Restated, the principle says that a relatively small percentage of the factors in any situation will be responsible for a relatively large percentage of effect. A few examples:

- Of all the items in a mail-order catalog, a small fraction of them, generally 10 to 20 percent, will account for a large percentage of the sales, generally 75 to 80 percent.
- A small percentage of employees will account for the majority of personnel problems, such as accidents and absences.
- A small percentage of quality characteristics will account for the bulk of customer complaints.
- A small percentage of customers will account for the bulk of sales volume.

Juran refers to the items that account for the bulk of any effect as "the vital few." They must be dealt with on an individual basis. The rest he originally called "the trivial many," although he later amended the description to "the useful many." These factors do not warrant individual attention and should be dealt with as a class. There is, Juran also admits, an "awkward zone" of factors that have more effect than the many, but not as much as the few. The Pareto Principle has come to be known, colloquially, as the 80-20 rule and has proved to have a broad application in business. Although it sounds obvious, even intuitive, the Pareto Principle is especially useful in businesses and industries where a huge number of variables can be contributing to any effect and where there is little, if any, agreement about which one is the most significant.

The first step in applying the Pareto Principle is to separate the vital few from the useful many by listing problems in order of their importance. This generally requires the gathering of data, some of which may already exist, some of which may need to be acquired. "Very few people have a list of their problems," says Juran. "And very few of those have the items listed in order of importance." Armed with knowledge of what the most important factors are, a business manager can implement a program of change and improvement that has the highest likelihood of delivering significant effect. "If we restrict our effort solely to the vital few, such effort is still generally successful, though it ignores the trivial many. In contrast, our effort, if applied solely to the trivial many, is always a failure."

In controlling quality, the Pareto Principle enables the manager to identify the defects that account for the greatest percentage of product failures. The Japanese, after World War II, for example, identified vacuum tubes as the major cause of failure of their telephone systems, and attacked the manufacturing conditions that led to vacuum-tube defects. The Pareto Principle, however, is equally useful for strategic management decisions. For example, many companies carry large numbers of inventory items, often numbering in the tens of thousands. Management may decide to reduce the number of items, but must make the decision based on a Pareto analysis of which items contribute most to sales or to profits.

Juran named the Pareto Principle after Vilfredo Pareto (1848–1923), an Italian economist who investigated the distribution of income. Pareto found that, universally, most of any nation's wealth was in the hands of a few people; the majority of people lived in relative poverty. Pareto did not talk, however, of the 80-20 percent split. In the *Handbook,* Juran seemed to imply that Pareto had broadened his discovery beyond the distribution of wealth, when, in fact, he hadn't. Another economist, M. O. Lorenz, was also partially responsible for the refinement of the Pareto Principle. In an article printed in the *Journal*

Figure 6.1 A small percentage of people hold a dispro-
portionately large percentage of wealth, said Lorenz.

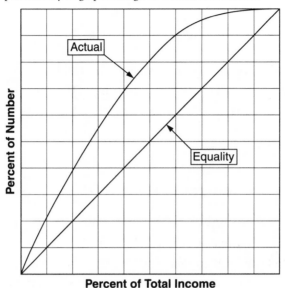

Percent of Total Income

of the American Statistical Association (June 1905), Lorenz offered a
graphical method (Figure 6.1) of showing the distribution of wealth.

Juran later confessed his error in attribution (Lorenz should have
gotten more credit), but claims that it was he who universalized this
useful principle. "Had I been structured along different lines, assuredly
I would have called it the Juran Principle. However, I was not structured that way. Yet I did need a shorthand designation, and I had no
qualms about Pareto's name. Hence the Pareto Principle."

Mobilizing for Breakthrough in Knowledge

Juran then explores the organizational structures that can be deployed
to guide the breakthrough process. Two "arms" are required.

1. The Steering Arm directs the acquisition and use of new
   knowledge.

2. The Diagnostic Arm does the detailed work of fact collection analysis.

Breakthrough in Knowledge—Diagnosis

Now the diagnostic arm goes out into the field and brings back its findings. These are talked out, resulting in further directions and further detailed studies. This goes on and on until the new knowledge needed for action has been acquired. At this stage, breakthrough in knowledge has been achieved.

Resistance to Change—Cultural Patterns

Juran identifies two aspects of change: a technical, or technological, change and a social consequence of the technological change. Of the two, the more difficult to deal with is the social change. "The social change is such a big trouble maker," he writes, "that those involved in Breakthrough should understand thoroughly the nature of social change." Juran cites several examples of social consequences that can erupt in reaction to technical change, from the rejection of safety shoes because they looked too common, to the seemingly inscrutable behavior of the coil winders in the Hawthorne experiments.

He likens the manager who seeks to make a technical change without considering the social consequences to a bee smashing against a window, again and again.

> Those who have not been sensitized to the existence of the cultural pattern have much in common with the bee at the window. Here is a proposal, technically sound and economically useful. Yet nothing happens. Resistance consists of a mysterious roadblock here, a fool argument there, a wild-goose chase yonder. The advocate of the change may well conclude that there are enemies around, and he or she may get personal about it.

Juran might well have been talking about himself, a bee crashing into a glass ceiling at Western Electric headquarters in the late 1930s.

Apart from his own experience of cultural difficulties, Juran claims to have been awakened to the importance of culture by the book *Cultural Patterns and Technical Change* (1953) edited by the anthropologist Margaret Mead. Prepared by the World Federation for Mental Health, the book presents a survey of several nonindustrialized cultures and the often unexpected consequences that arise when well-meaning outside advisers and experts have attempted to introduce modern industrial methods or technologies, in the name of progress. The authors exhibit a great sensitivity to the physical and emotional relation of workers to their work. Their insights into these unsophisticated workers and their traditional tools are remarkably relevant to the issues surrounding work in the great factories of the 1920s, and even today:

> New tools are being introduced, whether in agriculture or industry, to save labor or to increase production, or to improve a product, but the change they effect often involves much more than this. Where technology is simple, the tool is an extension of the body; the shuttle elongates and refines the finger, the mallet is a harder and more powerful fist. The tool follows the rhythm of the body; it enhances and intensifies; but it does not replace and does not introduce anything basically different. But the machine is not body-patterned. It has its own existence, its own rhythm, to which man must submit. The woman at her handloom controls the tension of the weft by the feeling in her muscles and the rhythm of her body motion; in the factory she watches the loom, and acts at externally stated intervals, as the operations of the machine dictate them. When she worked at home, she followed her own rhythm, and ended an operation when she felt—by the resistance against the pounding mallet or the feel between her fingers—that the process was complete. In the factory she is asked to adjust her rhythm to that of the rhythm prescribed by the factory; to do things according to externally set time limits.

Mead and her colleagues, of course, explore issues well beyond the impact of technical change on the individual. One intriguing note, discussing the prevailing cultural attitudes in Japan, may have caught Juran's eye on the brink of his departure to that country:

> In Japan, when a business was losing money and there was not enough work for all the employees, the employer did not therefore dismiss them; he was responsible for them. (This was termed "feather-bedding" by the *New York Times,* when a financial adviser from the United States discovered that it was the pattern in government offices.)

As seriously as Juran regarded these cultural issues, and as affected as he purports to be by Mead's writing, he demonstrates less sensitivity toward the "people problems" than toward other issues of making and managing breakthrough. "In dealing with cultural patterns we are at our worst," he confided, "hampered as we are by our limited basic knowledge and by our own emotional involvement. We now leave the morass to set foot on the more solid ground of taking action."

Breakthrough in Performance—Action

Once the morass of humanity has been escaped, the breakthrough can be achieved. But, even so, it can be a "squirming, elusive result." There will be obstacles, backsliding, unexpected twists and turns in the road. Now what is needed is to stabilize the forward movement, in short, to gain *control.*

Control at the New Level

Once breakthrough has been made, the organization seeks to once again maintain control over the process or activity—whatever it might be.

Juran devotes the second segment of *Managerial Breakthrough* to the process of control. He admits that he devoted so much energy to explaining the breakthrough process that his exploration of control is the less compelling of the two. Control may simply be the less compelling idea, to engineers and to managers alike.

The control sequence is based on the feedback loop, which Juran says is "billions of years old" and is the method for a biological organism to control those elements that are important to its survival, such as body temperature. The feedback loop consists of:

1. A sensing device. It detects what is happening in an environment, and this information is delivered to.
2. A control center. Here, the incoming information is compared to a standard. If it does not meet the standard, an order for change or correction of some type is issued to.
3. A motor device, or effector. This device takes some action intended to bring the thing sensed into closer harmony with the standard.

Control is essential to creating products and services that (1) meet design specifications, (2) can be manufactured with as few defects and rejects as possible, and (3) perform as expected, with minimal failures in the field. Control is based on the understanding of variance that Shewhart defined; statistical methods are required to determine the standard variation for any process.

Both sequences—for breakthrough and for control—must be repeated over and over again during the life of a company. Seldom, however, does an organization experience companywide breakthrough or companywide control. Some areas, processes, products, people, and activities will be undergoing breakthrough; others will be in a state of control. From the macro view, however, the organization that perpetually seeks breakthrough—sometimes small, sometimes large—and institutionalizes the breakthroughs through control, is the company that, in total, steadily improves.

Breakthrough and control, according to Juran, "are part of one continuing cycle of events. It consists of alternating plateaus and gains

Figure 6.2 Periods of breakthrough and control alternate in a process of continuous improvement. (From J. M. Juran and F. M. Gryna, editors, *Juran's Quality Control Handbook* (4th ed.), 1988. New York: McGraw-Hill. Reproduced with permission of McGraw-Hill Companies.)

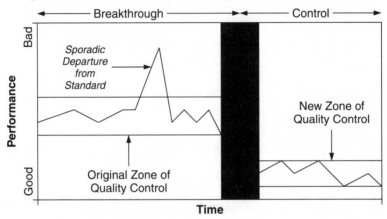

in performance. The plateaus are the result of Control—prevention of change. The gains are the result of Breakthrough—creation of Change. This goes on and on." He depicts the relationship of breakthrough and control as shown in Figure 6.2.

7

The Desperate Decade
(1979–1990)

American managers flailed away, because they honestly didn't know what to do.

J. M. Juran

JAPAN TAKES OFF

In large part, during the 1950s and 1960s, American senior managers were not listening to Juran, to Deming, to Armand Feigenbaum (advocate of Total Quality Control), or to other quality
advocates. In those postwar years, American companies were producing an astonishing percentage of all the world's manufactured goods,
as much as 50 percent. Juran's message to these fabulously successful
American managers—that they could and should improve quality by
using quality methods—implied that what they were already doing
wasn't good enough. But they were dominating world markets, with
sales booming and profits rising. "When you're making half of everything in the world, when you're the most productive society the world
has ever seen—not just at that point in time, but ever—who can tell
you you're doing anything wrong?" asked Blan Godfrey, chairman of
the Juran Institute. So, for years, quality was a subject striving to make
itself known outside the factory, beyond the purviews of the engineers and manufacturing managers. It took a crisis to propel quality
out of the factory and into the minds of America's senior managers.

That crisis was the rise of Japan as an industrial competitor. "Only
two years ago, America's international economic position seemed im-
pregnable," wrote Peter Drucker in a *Harvard Business Review* article
called "This Competitive World," in March 1961. He argued that the
world economy had become competitive for the first time since 1913
(or maybe 1929), and that "everyone in the Free World can get anything he wants—and can pay for—in the quantity and quality he
wants, from a number of different suppliers, and in a number of different countries." But most American managers, warned Drucker, were
not prepared for competition in the worldwide market. "Any American businessman, especially a manufacturer, should gauge the effectiveness and the efficiency of his business by its ability to compete in
the world." Drucker goes further, suggesting that even manufacturers

who do no exporting and compete only at home should be asking themselves, "What will I have to do to make my product capable of competing in the Japanese market?" If American companies could not compete in the world market, eventually a foreign competitor would appear to compete with them on their home turf. He argued against the use of protectionist measures, such as tariffs and against moving production to low-wage countries; rather, he said, "There is no way out but to restore U.S. competitive edge and product leadership." He contended that our competitors had had to learn how to do just that, and that Americans "usually supplied the textbooks. Now, we have to learn a few lessons ourselves."

Drucker was not the only observer who saw, early on, the role Japan would play in the global business environment. Deming claims that he predicted Japan's success as early as his trips there in 1950; he certainly believed in Japan in a way that few people did at that time. In April 1966, Juran revisited Japan, and was astonished at the industrial progress he found there. In particular, he was introduced to a phenomenon called the Quality Control Circle, or QC Circle. Although it had grown out of the teachings of Sarasohn, Deming, Juran, and Drucker, nothing quite like it existed in America; it was of Japanese invention.

Juran says that Quality Control Circles first appeared in 1962, as an extension of the efforts made during the 1950s to improve quality by managerial means. "By 1962," writes Juran, "it seemed logical to extend QC training to workers and to use teams of workers to achieve further improvements, as well as to broaden the extent of worker participation in the affairs of the company." The QC Circles, Juran learned on his visit in 1966, had achieved substantial cost savings and quality improvements in companies throughout Japan. Each Circle had averaged savings of $3,000; the 10,000 circles in existence had collectively achieved $30 million in improvements. Even allowing for all kinds of inconsistencies and inflations in measurement and reporting, the very fact that so many Circles existed and that so many people seemed convinced of their effectiveness caused Juran to conclude that the results were "astounding." Most remarkable was the makeup of these Circles. They were small groups; some had as few as three members, all of whom were workers, members of the nonsupervisor class. Membership in a QC Circle was voluntary. Most of the work was conducted outside of regular working hours, and compensation was often at lower-than-normal wages, if given at all.

Juran was so impressed that, in June 1966, following his visit to Japan, he decided to introduce the idea to his colleagues in Europe. During a lecture to the European Organization for Quality Control, held in Stockholm, Juran departed from his prepared text to describe the QC phenomenon he had witnessed the month before. The audience was intrigued, and a panel discussion was quickly formed to address the QC Circle issue; Ishikawa, Noguchi, and Imaizumi, as well as Juran, were among the panelists. According to Juran, it turned out to be "the high point of the conference." So, while Drucker was forewarning his readers about the coming global economy, Juran was describing the methods that the Japanese, in particular, would use to compete within it. Perhaps most intriguing, Juran comments that, "At this special session, and in the corridor discussions thereafter, it became evident that no one envisioned readily how to make the QC Circle concept effective in any other culture. It is amazing that such should be the universal reaction." The Japanese method was obviously successful; it clearly had achieved results in Japan. But like the Japanese in 1949 and 1950, listening to American experts explain the U.S. methods, it was difficult for the attendees of this European Conference to understand how QC concepts could be applied to their businesses in their own cultures.

Juran went on to make much broader statements about the position of Japan in the world economy. At the Stockholm conference—and in subsequent lectures in America, Sweden, and Yugoslavia—Juran was willing to state that "no other nation is so completely unified on the importance of good quality achievement, so eager to discover and adopt the best practices being followed in other countries, so avid in training all company levels and functions in modern methods of controlling quality, so vigilant in regulating the quality of exported goods." In short, said Juran, "The Japanese are headed for world quality leadership, and will attain it in the next two decades because no one else is moving there at the same pace."

It was as if a teacher suddenly had come in contact with a former student who had internalized the teacher's lessons and made them his own, and now was set to challenge the teacher with them. In 1966, Juran seemed astonished at what had happened. To this day, he seems unwilling or unable to assess exactly what effect he had on the Japanese miracle. In a paper published in 1967, Juran mused about what had contributed to the QC Circle phenomenon. "To a Westerner, the most astonishing aspect of the QC Circles has nothing to do with quality control. What is astonishing is the degree to which the Japanese have succeeded in harnessing the energy, ingenuity, and enthusiasm of the workforce to the unsolved problems of the company." It was completely unlike the work situation in the West, which was dominated by Taylorism (the worker is not expected to think) and unionism, and the adversarial relationships so often associated with unions. "Of utmost importance is the fact that, through the QC Circles, the Japanese have made a clean break with a tired, outworn theory which plagues the West. This is the theory that the company's quality troubles are due to operator indifference, blunder and even sabotage. Under this theory, the operators could solve the company's quality problems if only the right motivational lever could be found and thrown."

It did not take two decades for Japan to put America into crisis. By the mid-1970s, by Juran's estimate, Japan had caught up to the West in terms of quality and began rapidly to surpass us in some industries, particularly automobile manufacture and consumer electronics. (See Figure 7.1.)

The important aspect of Juran's observation was the *rate* of improvement. Although, according to Juran, the West was also improving the quality of its products and services during the postwar period, it was doing so at an evolutionary rate. Japan's businesses, on the other hand, were improving at a revolutionary rate. The financial

Figure 7.1   The quality of Japanese-manufactured product drew equal with that of the West in about 1975, says Juran. (Reprinted by permission from J. M. Juran, editor, *A History of Managing for Quality: The Evolution, Trends, and Future Directions of Managing for Quality*, 1995. Milwaukee: ASQC Quality Press.)

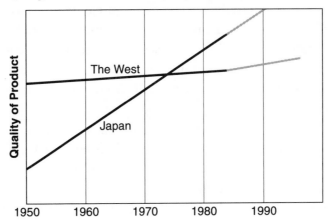

measurements used by American managers, however, failed to show this trend. The key measuring instruments were not designed to register issues related to quality; the money measurements—market share, sales growth, unit growth, profits, ROI, and so on—indicated that things were fine. Not until their financial instrument panels began to register problems did American managers truly hear the case for quality.

The early indicators of what was happening came in two industries that involve precision mass manufacture:

1. Consumer electronics, especially color television manufacture. Primarily as a result of competition from Japanese manufacturers, the number of U.S. makers of color televisions dwindled from a high of twenty-five to just one.

2. Automobiles. The domestic market share of the America's three major auto-makers was sharply reduced by competition from the Japanese.

Only then did American managers snap to attention and begin to look for solutions to the problem. Juran watched as America adopted various strategies to respond to the worldwide competitive threat. One strategy was to try to protect the American market by keeping imports out, particularly automobiles. Tariffs, import quotas, accusations of dumping, imprecations against the Japanese motives, and appeals to American patriotism to "Buy American" were all implemented. Another solution seemed to lie in increased inspection—the old method of ensuring quality: "Try to keep the bad products from going out to the customers." That, too, had some effect, but it is a costly way to improve quality. So, managers flailed away, says Juran, "because they honestly didn't know what to do. They had been detached from the subject for years and years. They had delegated it to the quality departments. And being detached, they didn't know what to do." All these actions had some effect, but they did not address the real problem, nor did they provide a real remedy. The solution was to become competitive, which meant mastering both aspects of quality.

1. Control quality. Stop making defective products.
2. Achieve breakthroughs in quality.

The crisis provoked by Japanese competition affected American businesspeople in the same way that the postwar crisis (although of vastly greater severity) had affected their Japanese counterparts: They went scurrying for advice.

Marketing the Knowledge

For years, Juran had resisted the urgings of his colleagues to build an organization. He had left Western Electric because he had concluded that he did not belong in a large organization; nothing had transpired to change his mind about that assessment of his own nature. Besides, he was enjoying a personal and professional freedom that few people attain.

At the age of 70, when most people have retired or are wishing they could, Juran's schedule had gotten more hectic than it had ever been. In an article published in 1975, Juran indulged in a public summation of his activities during the previous year. In 1974, he writes, he took six extended trips to fourteen countries, including Norway, Germany, Finland, Israel, Australia, Japan, Hong Kong, Taiwan, and the Philippines. A total of more than 100,000 air miles traveled and more than half the year's weeks spent on the road. And yet, he reckoned that he was at home more than most of his "employed contemporaries. What makes this possible is the ingenious device of having no conventional 'office,' i.e., my study is part of our apartment. My journey from breakfast to 'work' is 20 meters long and is made on foot."

Also in 1974, the third edition of the *Handbook* was published and the Romanian, Polish, and Japanese editions of *Quality Planning and Analysis* appeared. He estimated that, in 1974 alone, nearly 6,000 people had attended his courses, seminars, and lectures, and that he had sold a total of some 17,000 books. He addressed managers in Oslo; lectured at the Sydney Opera House; conducted a course at the China Productivity Center. He engaged in a "modicum of consulting." And he tasted the varied pleasures of the traveling life: restaurants, museums, concerts, sightseeing. He concluded: "I would be mad to give up so fascinating a way of life."

Nevertheless, the demand for his services had outpaced his capacity to speak, travel, write, and consult. The amount of knowledge he possessed could not be captured even in the massive *Handbook*. Companies and organizations were clamoring for help, and the demand for training, which he had long advocated, was on the increase, bringing with it an increased need for training materials. There were indications, here and there, that video could be a powerful tool for education and training, and that video players were becoming sufficiently ubiquitous within organizations to make educational video programs commercially viable, even lucrative. Videos could also bring his ideas to a much wider audience than he could reach in person, and in a different and more emotionally engaging way than his books could achieve.

When Juran explored the possibility of creating a video series with various book publishing houses, they offered him the standard 15 percent royalty. That seemed like a bad deal, considering the amount of effort involved and the limited experience of publishing companies with video production. Although he disliked the idea of establishing an organization, Juran began to mull over the idea of creating a small company specifically to produce training materials. He had no intention of establishing a management consultancy and had no interest in running a company; he refused to allow another organization to dominate his life, as Western Electric had. What he needed was an energetic manager.

A bizarre family adventure brought Juran in contact with Howland Blackiston, a young man with a successful career in advertising. In 1979, Juran and his wife were living in New York City. Juran had long been estranged from his eldest son, Robert, who had experienced a rash of difficulties, emotional and otherwise, throughout his life. Robert had fathered a child when he was very young, and the child had been adopted at age three. Juran had established trust funds for all his grandchildren, but had lost track of Robert's daughter. In the late 1970s, Juran set out to find her and eventually located her. Now named Joy Grozinger, she was living in a small apartment in Florida, struggling to become a theatrical costume designer. When Juran offered to bring her to New York and subsidize her, she accepted and came to live with the Jurans at their apartment at UN Plaza. In New York, Joy met Howland Blackiston through a mutual friend. Blackiston began to court Joy; soon Juran was obliquely courting Blackiston. As creative director at a Manhattan advertising agency, Blackiston was deeply involved in production and creative direction and the communications process. He knew nothing about the quality movement and had never heard of

Dr. Juran. Juran, on the other hand, knew nothing about video and cared little for marketing.

Over Sunday brunches, the two discussed the ins and outs of video production and distribution. Juran hired Blackiston on a freelance basis to do some research, which involved attending a few of Juran's AMA classes and analyzing the market for videos. How many companies had video players? What subjects might they be interested in? Juran and Blackiston determined that it would cost about a million dollars to create a series of tapes that would achieve a quality standard equal to that of television broadcast news. Juran had the million, and Blackiston, who was 28 at the time, had the energy and desire to take a risk.

Blackiston took the gamble. Juran Enterprises was founded, and Blackiston was installed in a large office at UN Plaza. They set about creating a series of tapes that would be called *Juran on Quality Improvement*. At that time, few training videos were available for business audiences, and virtually nothing could be found on the subject of quality. Blackiston, looking for models, found tapes by a statistician, Stuart Hunter of Princeton University, and a recent entry to the market, a tape on negotiating by Dr. Chester L. Karrass. To Blackiston's eye—trained in advertising and accustomed to commercial production values—the style of most of the videos on the market was unacceptable. Some were little more than recorded lectures—shot in black and white, with inadequate lighting, jerky camera movement, and scratchy sound.

Juran wrote a script for a pilot video, *Quality Improvement and Cost Reduction*. They worked for months trying to establish a style that would be appealing and marketable, and would also accommodate Dr. Juran's speaking style. The first test video was shot on a set designed to look like a study, with Juran staring down his nose at his script. They showed the video to seminar attendees and got negative reactions. They shot a second test, this one with Juran using an overhead projector, as was his custom. Audiences thought it was worse than the first. They shot three more tests, working through issue after issue, with Juran rankling over the demands of the unfamiliar medium, and Blackiston trying diplomatically to work him toward an acceptable product. Juran didn't want to wear makeup. He didn't think it mattered what clothing he wore. He wanted to use an over-head projector or a blackboard. He didn't want a TelePrompTer. Blackiston's cause was helped when Juran called his brother, Nathan, for advice. Nathan had had a long career in Hollywood, first as a set designer (he won an Academy Award in 1941 for Art Direction on John Ford's *How Green Was My Valley*) and then as a director of B-movies. "Do one show and get it right," he counseled, "before you shoot the whole series."

Five tests later, they finally settled on a style. Juran appeared in his dark suit and signature black bow tie behind a podium. He read from a TelePrompTer and, as he did, wrote brief bits of text and drew sim-ple visuals with a marker on a flat, glass surface set into the podium, similar in nature to the writing surface of an overhead projector. Juran's jottings then appeared on a video screen behind him. The tech-nique provided Juran with his accustomed activity of writing, which helped him pace his presentation. Once the style was determined, they produced the entire series of tapes—sixteen in all—consuming some $700,000 in the process. They also changed the name of the company from Juran Enterprises to Juran Institute, to convey a less commercial and more academic impression to prospective customers.

During production, Blackiston and an assistant began to send out letters to potential buyers—a mailing list of more than 2,000 people who had attended Juran's seminars and courses over the years. Initial reaction was strong; some bought the program before it was com-pleted. The series was launched in January 1981. For the purchase price of $15,000, the buyer received the 16 tapes, along with a library of Juran's published books. Workbooks cost extra. The orders starting rolling in. "It was just delicious," remembers Blackiston, "the money that was coming in was positively golden. We were selling one of those a day. If a week went by that we hadn't sold five or six or seven, we'd get depressed." The video series remained the backbone of the Juran

Institute for several years, producing some $30 million in sales. Black-iston (who married Joy in 1978) is president of Juran Institute at this writing.

A BOOM IN THE ADVICE BUSINESS

Juran on Quality Improvement appeared on the market at a most auspicious time. Although Juran was one of the first to reach the market with video training tapes, he was not the first to expose the nation to the idea of quality through the television medium. Just as he had in Japan, W. Edwards Deming once again preceded Juran. In June 1980, Deming had been featured in an NBC television documentary called *If Japan Can . . . Why Can't We?* It focused on the issue of productivity, both in Japan and in the United States, and argued persuasively, if in a rather oversimplified, stentorian fashion, that Japan was beating America and that something was fundamentally wrong with America. The last several minutes or so featured a then obscure expert in statistical process control named W. Edwards Deming. For Deming the documentary marked "the turning point between academic obscurity and public fame," according to Lloyd Dobyns and Clare Crawford-Mason, respectively a reporter and the producer on the show.

Deming did "most of the teaching" in Japan, the voice-over declares. And then appears a bald, old man—Deming was 79 at the time—who seems to be a cross between an eccentric professor and an impassioned preacher. He seems unshakably sure of himself as he derides American management, saying, "I think people here expect miracles. American management thinks that they can just copy from Japan. But they don't know what to copy." He also assures the audience that we, too, can be as productive and successful as the Japanese have been.

The program generated a huge response. It was as if the nation had caught a glimpse of the mastermind who had created the monster—

Japan—that was nipping at America's heels. "Those of us involved with the program did not understand its potential impact. None of us was prepared for the requests for transcripts and copies of the programs. We had not budgeted for any of it. I am told that the network still gets request for copies and transcripts," says Dobyns. For Deming, the program provided an avalanche of business. "Our phones rang off the hook. Dr. Deming's mail quadrupled, and beyond," remembers his longtime secretary, Cecelia Killian. The television program made Deming a household name and helped to focus the attention of the United States on the issue of quality.

Juran had been invited to participate in the NBC documentary. Blackiston received a call from an NBC researcher several weeks prior to the broadcast, asking for an interview with Juran. To Blackiston, then preparing the video series for sale, the prospect of Juran appearing on a major television show was "a marketer's dream." At their next meeting, Blackiston brought up the request with Juran. "I said, NBC wants to interview you," Blackiston remembers. "And he said no. It's those journalists, he said. I don't need an interview. I don't need the publicity. They always get it all wrong and I'm too busy. Tell them no. So we turned them down." According to Dobyns, "I remember Juran saying that it was obvious from the researcher's questions that we had already settled on Dr. Deming."

Whether Juran would have been included in the final cut of the show if he had participated, and whether he then would have made an impact similar to Deming's, are imponderables. But, despite the fact that Juran was not included, the broadcast helped pave the way for acceptance of his video series.

As a result of the documentary, Deming became a household name. He found himself besieged with requests to serve as a speaker and sought after as an adviser to some of the nation's largest manufacturers, including General Motors and The Ford Motor Company. He was showered with honorary doctorates—fifteen of his total of sixteen were awarded from 1983 to 1993, the year he died.

Deming's work and ideas fomented a host of articles and books. Deming's own book, *Quality, Productivity, and Competitive Position* was published in 1982 and updated as *Out of the Crisis,* in 1986. A flood of books about him followed. In *The Deming Management Method* (1986), reporter Mary Walton called Deming "the genius who revitalized Japanese industry." Two more Deming paeans appeared in 1990: *Dr. Deming, The American Who Taught the Japanese About Quality,* by Rafael Aguayo, and *The Man Who Discovered Quality, How W. Edwards Deming Brought the Quality Revolution to America,* by Andrea Gabor. Crawford-Mason and Dobyns produced a sequel to *If Japan Can . . . Why Can't We?* called *Quality or Else,* which aired on the Public Broadcasting System in 1991. That same year, Deming was featured in a *Fortune* Magazine article called *25 Who Help the U.S. Win.* It declared Deming to be "the world's preeminent quality master" and a "prophet long ignored in his own land." As of this writing, more than twenty books that concern Deming and his ideas are still in print.

But Deming was not the only quality advocate who achieved fame and fortune in the 1980s. As much as Blackiston and Juran were aware of Deming and his rising prominence, they considered their main competitor to be Philip Crosby. Crosby became well known with the publication of his book, *Quality Is Free,* in 1979, and he founded his company, Philip Crosby Associates (PCA) in the same year. PCA grew at a faster rate than Juran Institute, climbing from $400,000 in revenues the first year to $8 million in 1982. In 1983, Crosby was approached by General Motors to conduct seminars for their management. "I suggested that working with GM could be a problem for us because we would have to build up our staff in order to handle them and they might change their mind suddenly. They offered to purchase an equity position in our company in order to make things more permanent." Crosby received $4 million in return for 10 percent of PCA.

PCA continued to grow, reaching nearly $35 million in 1985, when Crosby took his company public. At that time, Crosby reckons he was delivering some 75 speeches per year, jetting from engagement to engagement in his Lear 55 aircraft, receiving fees ranging from $10,000 to $15,000 per day. (Juran commanded similar fees at the time.) PCA, like Juran Institute, produced and marketed videos and workbooks, in addition to running the PCA Quality College for managers. In 1989, Crosby sold PCA, of which he owned a little less than 10 percent at the time, to the Alexander Proudfoot Company, a consulting firm listed on the London Stock Exchange, for $60 million. Today, Crosby continues to operate under the name Career IV, dividing his time between Altamonte Springs, Florida, and Highlands, North Carolina. He writes books and other materials such as CD-ROMs and speaks to audiences all over the world at a standard fee of $15,000 per engagement—in nations that include India, Chile, Greece, and Indonesia.

Crosby's style is sharply different from those of Juran and Deming. His approach has a strong base of religious faith, and he presents a no-nonsense, regular-guy image, which, coupled with a pride in his own success, is appealing and accessible. Unlike Juran the engineer and lawyer and Deming the mathematical physicist, there is nothing of the scholar or pedant about Crosby. He comes across as a plain-speaking American business manager, very much like the plain-speaking business managers in his audience. Crosby's detractors, which include Juran, tend to characterize him as a sloganizer. He receives the most criticism for his concept of Zero Defects:

> To eliminate this waste, to improve the operation, to become more efficient, we must concentrate on preventing the defects and errors that plague us. The defect that is prevented doesn't need repair, examination, or explanation.
>
> The first step is to examine and adopt the attitude of defect prevention. This attitude is called, symbolically: Zero Defects. Zero Defects is a standard for management, a standard that management can convey to the employees to help them to decide to "do the job right the first time."

Crosby's contention that quality is "not only free, it is an honest-to-everything profit maker," sounded extremely appealing to American business managers. To Juran and other thoughtful quality practitioners, it was a misleading statement that encouraged some managers to expect fabulous results with little effort. Crosby even went so far as to promise: "If you concentrate on making quality certain, you can probably increase your profit by an amount equal to 5 to 10 percent of your sales. That is a lot of money for free." Crosby's own version of the quality improvement process involves fourteen steps. Unlike the Shewhart/Deming cycle and Juran's breakthrough sequence, Crosby's fourteen steps are prescriptive in a rather inflexible way. They offer a plan for instituting a quality program, rather than embedding the quality process into the mind of an organization.

To Juran, who had spent years exploring the cost implications of quality (higher quality of conformance could reduce costs, higher quality of design generally costs more) and articulating a universal sequence for breakthrough that could be applied and adapted to any process in any organization, the Crosby approach seemed superficial and even deceptive. Crosby says that his work was never about slogans and that he has been wrongly characterized. "My book was the first book on quality without a chart in it," he says, differentiating himself from the engineers. And that's why, Crosby believes, managers took to it.

Juran had a low opinion of much of the advice-giving activities of the 1980s. Too many were designed, he said, to "stir up the animals. Put up the banners, shout the slogans, and otherwise go into exhortation to urge people to do better. We went through maybe a decade of that. It just did a lot of damage and created a lot of divisiveness in the companies." Juran didn't think much of NBC's *If Japan Can . . . Why Can't We?* either. He felt that it touted statistical process control, which had little to do with quality. "In 1980, there emerged a widely viewed videocast, *If Japan Can . . . Why Can't We?*," he wrote. "It concluded that Japanese quality was due to their use of statistical methods taught to them by Deming. This conclusion had little relation to reality; however, the program was cleverly presented and was persuasive to many viewers." He stated his distaste more bluntly to reporter Lloyd Dobyns, saying that the program had "set the quality movement back five years."

By 1993, Juran was tired of the debate over who did what, when, and why in Japan. "Let me clear up for good one bit of chauvinist nonsense," he wrote in *Harvard Business Review:*

> In the minds of some journalists and industrialists, Japan's world leadership in product quality is the result of the lectures given four decades ago by two Americans—W. Edwards Deming and Joseph M. Juran. Had Deming and I not given those lectures, these people insist, Japanese goods would still be of stone-age quality. In my view there is not a shred of truth to such assertions. Had Deming and I stayed home, the Japanese would have achieved world quality leadership all the same. We did provide a jump start, without which the Japanese would have been put to more work—and the job might have taken longer—but they would still be ahead of the United States in the quality revolution.

But even the media stars of the quality movement, Crosby and Deming, were eclipsed by a general management consultant, Tom Peters, co-author (with Robert H. Waterman) of *In Search of Excellence,* which appeared in October 1982. The book sold a million copies in its first year, and, as of 1996, had sold some five million. *In Search of Excellence,* which appeared amid considerable public discussion (to which the NBC broadcast had contributed) about America's problems and Japan's successes, delivered a refreshingly positive message: "The findings from the excellent companies amount to an upbeat message. There is good news from America. Good management practice today is not resident only in Japan." In *The Witch Doctors,* John Micklethwait and Adrian Woolridge write of *In Search of Excellence:* "The book seemed perfectly designed to appeal to an America that was worried about its declining competitiveness but tired of being told about the Japanese miracle." There was plenty of gloom and worry to be had from other observers. For example: "In business, as in other areas of our national life, we seem to experience a chronic lack of motivation, a failure of will," wrote Frank Gibney in *Miracle by Design*. "What is wrong with us? And what are we doing to remedy it?" In Deming's own book, *Out of the Crisis,* he commented, "With the storehouse of skills and knowledge contained in its millions of unemployed, and with the even more appalling underuse, misuse and abuse of skills and knowledge in the army of employed people in all ranks in all industries, the United States may be today the most underdeveloped nation in the world."

Peters's message, and particularly his tone, differed significantly from that of the quality experts. Their ideas (even Crosby's) had emerged from the world of engineering and were focused on methods and measurements; Peters celebrated the human, often irrational, drivers of business success. The ideas were exciting, the language was colloquial, the book fast-paced, and the author was youthful. Peters was 40 at publication; Deming was 81, Juran 77, Drucker 71.

The book's success—and the endless stream of Peters books, articles, seminars, lectures, talk-show appearances, interviews, audio tapes and videos that followed—served to create a whole new character on the business stage: the guru. Not only did Peters create the character, he made himself a star, and, in turn, brought a new glamour and status to the world of business. As Peter Drucker remarked, "When Aunt Mary has to give that nephew of hers a high school graduation present and she gives him *In Search of Excellence* you know that management has become part of the general culture."

VALUE, QUALITY, AND THE LANGUAGE OF MONEY

With all the concern about America's lack of competitiveness and all the noise about how to solve the problem—in the media, in the literature, and from the pronouncements of the gurus—many of the big corporate ships began to seek a course toward quality. Their methods were varied; their results, uneven. Some companies did little more than adopt the slogans of quality, drape the factory walls in banners, and run every employee through a prefabricated course on quality improvement. Some companies chose to align themselves with a quality guru. The most successful ones approached the issue seriously, studied the literature, invited more than one expert to talk with them. They purchased and consumed the prepared educational materials—books, workbooks, videos, seminars. Then they assimilated the ideas, developed their own programs and methods, and embedded quality into the thinking and style of their organization. This approach has become so prevalent today that the major competitor to the consulting firms, especially in quality improvement, is the client itself. They have learned how to implement and manage quality for themselves. Generally, companies focused on Juran's second definition of quality—quality of conformance, or "freedom from deficiencies"—because it offered the quickest way to show results, by cutting costs through the prevention of rework and reduction of waste. The idea of extracting "free gold" that lay, untouched, in the mine of manufacturing was very appealing. Fewer managers grasped the other definition of quality—as a collection of features that provide customer satisfaction—or, they took longer to understand it. Few immediately connected the idea of quality with breakthrough, a process that could propel a company into new products and new markets, and thus increase sales. The essential problem, Juran knew, was the same one he had confronted for years: Managers talked a different language than did engineers and manufacturers, and they lived by a different system of measurements.

"There is no true value of anything," wrote W. Edwards Deming in his foreword to Walter Shewhart's book, *Statistical Method from the Viewpoint of Quality Control.* Deming was using the word *value* in its mathematical sense, although it applies perfectly well to the sense of "worth" that is common to business in the 1990s. Deming explained further: "There is, instead, a figure that is produced by application of a master or ideal method of counting or of measurement. This figure may be accepted as a standard until the method of measurement is supplanted by experts in the subject matter with some other method and some other figure. There is no true value of the speed of light; no true value of the number of inhabitants within the boundaries of (e.g.) Detroit."

In other words, nothing can be measured exactly. Any measurement is affected by the method used and will inevitably be replaced by some new method and some new value at some time in the future. This idea underlies Shewhart's declaration that the activity of mass manufacture of interchangeable parts, which he dates to 1787 (although Juran puts it at 1789), had been founded on the concept of exact science, "according to which an attempt was made to produce piece parts to exact dimensions." Engineers and manufacturing managers, finding it impossible to produce any quantity of piece parts to exactly the same dimensions, abandoned the pursuit of perfection in favor of the use of tolerances. So long as the finished part fell within specified dimensions or amounts, it was acceptable for use. Thus, says Shewhart, "whereas the concept of mass production of 1787 was born of an exact science, the concept underlying the quality control chart technique of 1924 was born of a probable science."

Over the years, engineers and manufacturing people developed a language of their own, "the language of things" as Juran calls it. It is concerned with materials, parts, units, products, and shipments. At the same time, business owners and managers developed another language for measuring the value of their business—finance, or "the language of money." It talks of sales, profit, investment, and return. Early in his career, Juran recognized that most organizations speak these two completely different languages and realized that the people in between—middle managers who deal with people on the shop floor and in the executive suites—must become bilingual. They must learn to translate the language of things into the language of money for the benefit of their managers. And, they must learn to translate strategic

financial objectives into the language of things for the benefit of those
on the shop floor, an equally daunting task.

In a paper presented to the Society of Statistical Quality Control
and the Society for Advancement of Management, in April 1945,
Juran said, "To the manager, the problems of quality usually appear as
tangible, measurable things. He has losses in defectives, scrap and junk
running into many thousands of dollars, possibly into millions of dollars. The sum of the measurable things—the payroll of the inspection
force, the junk bill, the scrap bill, the cost of rework, the cost of the
customers' returns—the sum of these measurable things is the size of
the gold mine in which the Inspection Engineer would dig. Unless
this mine is demonstrably large enough to pay for the cost of digging,
there will very likely be no digging." Knowing that quality had to be
explained in terms of money, Juran had long worked to convince senior managers of the tremendous opportunity for cost savings represented by the "freedom from deficiencies" definition of quality.

The Quality Message Seeps
into the Executive Suite

In company after company, Juran said to the senior executives what
their engineers and manufacturing personnel knew and had been trying to say for years. In the late 1960s, for example, Juran was invited
to conduct a seminar for a number of managers and engineers of Rolls-
Royce Aero Engine Division at the University of Nottingham in
England. While there, the Chairman and Chief Executive, Sir Den-
ning Pearson, asked Juran to take a look at their manufacturing operations. Juran did so, and discovered a tremendous amount of waste—as
much as 30 percent of what Rolls made never got to the customer. It
had to be reworked or scrapped. Juran worked with the factory managers to estimate the cost of this "gold in the mine." "It was a shock-
ing amount," says Juran, "all the way through. No exceptions." Juran

presented his findings to Pearson, who blanched when he heard the staggering sum that his factories were throwing down the drain. But, Juran told him, using their existing technological and managerial capabilities, they probably could cut the amount of waste in half within a few years. Juran told him, "There would be some effort to do that, but the return on investment would be much greater than selling aircraft engines." Pearson was immensely impressed by the idea that reducing waste through quality improvement could provide a greater financial gain than any other activity the company was pursuing at the time.

Pearson asked Juran to make his presentation again, later that week. Juran did so, and then sat back to listen to an "absolutely fascinating discussion" among Pearson's staff. Here was an enormous opportunity and not only was nobody working on it, nobody even recognized it as such. "And then one of the directors came up with an observation that, as far as I was concerned, was one of these blinding flashes of illumination. He said that, in Rolls-Royce, the road to climbing the ladder is based on creating income, designing and selling aircraft engines. Those who are the most ambitious and want to do that are not going to get themselves involved in cost reduction in factories. That's lower grade work."

So, just as he had experienced Western Electric's attitude toward the too-short wires, Juran found cultural and organizational barriers to the understanding and pursuit of quality at Rolls-Royce. This continued to be the state of affairs at companies throughout the United States and around the world, throughout the 1960s and into the 1970s. The potential of the gold in the mine was still not sufficient to attract the attention of America's senior managers, so long as the measures they cared most about remained in good shape—market share, sales growth, profits, and return on investment.

Juran's ability to talk with senior managers, and to state the importance of quality in the language of money, enabled many of America's best-managed companies to connect with his ideas.

The experience at the Aluminum Company of America (Alcoa) was typical. Alcoa is a global maker of aluminum in a great variety of forms, including sheets for cans and packaging; plates for ships, aircraft, and cars; and engineered products, including rods, tubes and wire for all kinds of purposes. Ron Kegarise, Director of Quality Systems at Alcoa, had long been trying to enlist senior management in the quality effort. "I had a very difficult time convincing our senior management that they needed to embrace quality as a significant objective. They said, 'We understand quality. We understand it's important. But it's implied in our product.' " In other words, they were understanding quality in the "old" sense of the word, the Sloan sense of the word, as a matter of *grade*.

But, by 1982, Alcoa had gotten a taste of the crisis. Competition was intensifying. The company had battled through recession. "We started to say, 'We're big, we're powerful, and we're smart, and we have a lot of capital behind us, but we've got to start to do things differently. And it looks like quality is certainly one of the emerging features of the '80s.' Some of our folks in Pittsburgh, our corporate leaders, started to get very interested in quality and started to raise the banner and tried to get some better methodology. But at that particular time, there were not very many methodologies to latch onto."

Like many other companies, Alcoa first turned to statistical methods, and found them useful, but not enough. "We really needed to understand the rest of the quality tools, and to understand a methodology that fit our culture, which is strongly technical," recalls Kegarise. Some of the quality approaches that were considered had a strong anti-Taylor bias, and placed a heavy emphasis on the role of the worker. "I think the worker does a good job of being able to identify things that are wrong, to identify symptoms," says Kegarise. "But I don't necessarily believe that the worker can solve all the problems because some of the problems are much more technical in nature."

Alcoa went on an exhaustive search for a quality guru and reviewed the materials the quality advocates had available. "We were looking for someone to help us implement a quality revolution. We looked at Crosby, which was basically the only act in town at that time. We were turned off because it was that message that quality is free and it was the old zero defects idea. We'd lived through that. That was not very good." Alcoa also considered Deming, but felt that the philosophy of quality was already well understood. The company needed someone who could tell them *how to implement* a quality revolution, rather than explain the philosophy of quality. Then Alcoa heard about Juran. Kegarise summarized: "The thing we were impressed with was the fact that he had been a manager, he had been in industry, he had led departments. When he talks about quality, and talks about management, talks about managers, I believe him because he's been there."

From Juran, Alcoa learned some of the basics of quality, starting with the concept of variation. "That was a revelation to me," remembers Kegarise. "When I started with Alcoa, I solved the same mechanical problem on one of our alloys three times in one year. If I'd had more time, I probably would have solved it five times. The key is: I didn't solve it properly the first time. I just jumped to a conclusion. And now we've learned to solve these things properly. Sporadic problems are things we work on. They go away because of some fix we put in. But the problem is still latently there. And until we work in a chronic problem-solving mode, we're going to continue to have sporadic problems. Joe has really helped us focus in that area. It's kind of an awakening."

Motorola, too, looked to Juran for help. Again, the move to quality emerged in a rather vague way, in reaction to a sense that trouble was brewing. For Motorola, the shift came in 1979, according to Jack Germain, then the Corporate Director of Quality. "We had an officers' meeting where we talked about all aspects of the company. That's when we latched onto this idea: Maybe our quality is not the greatest. There are some disgruntled customers. Maybe we ought to be doing something about it in a very important way. And out of that meeting, came a number of things we decided to do differently. I was one of them." Germain was named Corporate Director of Quality. "They said, OK, Jack. You're the catalyst," says Germain. "And I thought, now what? We had the top guys all lined up to go do battle and say, let's make this a better company! But how do you get to 'better company?' What are we going to do to make us better? All those questions had to be raised, had to be written down. Then, we had to get answers for them. And then we had to go line up some 100,000 employees in at least 55 operations around the world, speaking at least eleven languages. Those were some of the dimensions of the problem. Egads!"

Motorola turned to the quality experts for help. "We must have talked to everybody who was an expert in this field, one way or another," says Germain. They found Juran the most useful because of his practical approach. "Unlike a lot of the other people, he taught you how to organize to solve problems so you could deal with the real things that a real improvement process had to cope with." In 1981, Motorola decided that "we were going to have a tenfold improvement in everything we did in five years. That created a situation for a lot of our people—they had to come to grips with very serious problems and they didn't know how to go about solving them. To have Juran, whom we considered the leading quality expert in the world, explaining it all on those tapes that we could ship around the world, was very significant to us."

Motorola went on to win the Malcolm Baldrige National Quality Award in 1988, with very little investment. "If we were to look at our own financial base and look where we made heavy investments to get quality improvement going at Motorola, we'd be hard pressed to find anything very significant." Improvements, however, were exceptional: a 50-to-1 to 100-to-1 return, reckons Germain. The company likes to say it saved $2 billion in the period from 1987 to 1990. And those gains stem from the reduction of defects and waste. Germain also credits Juran with helping Motorola achieve breakthrough improvement—better products that customers want. For example, Juran's ideas helped Motorola dramatically increase its market share for pocket paging systems in Japan, and achieve a leadership position. Motorola also significantly increased the quality and reliability of its cellular phone systems, using Juran's methodology.

THE JURAN TRILOGY

Such stories unfolded over and over again during the 1980s. Managers in company after company—engineers, general business managers, quality managers—were visited by revelations, small or large, that brought them to the idea of quality. It became clear, however, that a yawning gap existed between the idea of quality and the achievement of quality.

This may be why the Crosby approach—which sets high standards, prescribes companywide quality days, and talks generally about management style—is blamed for widening the gap, when, in fact, it may only have thrown it into more visible relief. Deming's approach, too, was strong on philosophy and exhortation, but less able to provide wisdom about how to organize and what to do when, with whom, and about what. In *Out of the Crisis,* Deming articulated the fourteen points that constituted his "theory of management," along with what he called the "seven deadly diseases" and a raft of obstacles that stood in the way of realizing the points. The points take the form of imperatives, such as "Institute Training" and "Drive Out Fear," which are provocative and useful but come with very little support about how they should be accomplished. In Juran's opinion, although Deming calls for the "elimination of slogans and exhortations," his fourteen points fall into the category of slogans. "If anybody else had come up with those, they would have been ignored," says Juran.

Juran gradually came to believe that an element was missing in his universal sequences for quality control and quality breakthrough. As senior managers began to listen to the quality message and commit themselves to quality management, they were also in need of a methodology—and it had to be articulated in the language Juran knew they understood best, finance. In May 1986, Juran presented a paper to the 40th Annual Quality Congress of the ASQC in Anaheim, California. In it, he declared that America was suffering a "crisis in quality" and that "our traditional ways are not adequate to deal with the quality crisis." We must "create a universal way of thinking about quality—a way applicable to all functions and to all levels in the hierarchy, from the chief executive officer to the worker in the office or the factory."

"Charting a new course," he said, "requires extensive personal leadership and participation by upper managers." And to gain that, we must "arm upper managers with experience and training in how to manage for quality." Juran's solution was to add a third piece to the methodology: quality planning. He called the trio the Juran Trilogy:

- Quality planning.
- Quality control.
- Quality improvement.

Juran laid out six steps for quality planning, which define the front end of the corporate process—the part that comes before there is a process in place to control or improve. The steps are:

1. Identify the customers, both external and internal.
2. Determine customer needs.
3. Develop product features that respond to customer needs.
4. Establish quality goals that meet the needs of customers and suppliers alike.
5. Develop a process that can produce the needed product features.
6. Prove process capability—prove that the process can meet the quality goals under operating conditions.

Juran argued that the three phases of the quality process were analogous to those of finance: (1) budgeting, (2) cost control, and, (3) cost reduction/profit improvement. And companies that practice all three aspects of quality, said Juran, will operate in a spiral of improvement (Figure 7.2).

Figure 7.2   The spiral of continuous improvement. (From J. M. Juran and F. M. Gryna, editors, *Juran's Quality Control Handbook* (4th ed.), 1988. New York: McGraw-Hill. Reproduced with permission of McGraw-Hill Companies.)

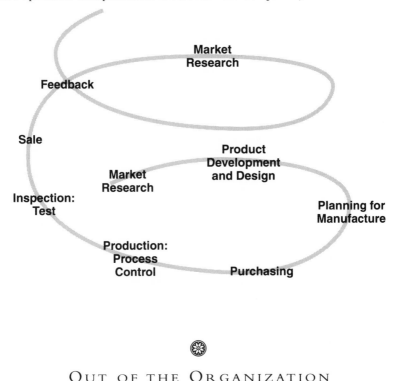

OUT OF THE ORGANIZATION

After nearly a decade of activity at the Juran Institute, Juran's longest tenure within a company since his time at Western Electric, he turned over the ownership of the Institute to its employees, stepped down, and assumed the title of Chairman Emeritus. He handed over the reins to A. Blanton Godfrey, a former client and an employee of his industrial alma mater, AT&T.

Juran turned to a "mountain of work" that he had been putting off for years, including family matters, guiding the Juran Foundation—which he had founded in 1986 to support the application of quality methods to environmental issues—and the writing of his autobiography.

8

Guru at the Dikes

Joe is like a river, he just flows on and on.

Lawrence Appley

THE QUALITY DIKES

I
n the 1980s, the new idea of quality—which had been taking root since the early part of the century—began to flower in our national consciousness, partly because it became more institutionalized, codified, and publicized than ever before. With the establishment of The Malcolm Baldrige National Quality Award in 1987 (Juran was a member of the Board of Overseers), the emergence of new quality standards (particularly the International Standards Organization's ISO 9000 Series), and, in the 1990s, Vice President Albert Gore's efforts to reinvent government using quality methods (Juran testified before the committee which Gore chaired), quality has become more and more recognized and validated as a useful pursuit.

Quality has taken root in business organizations in less formal ways as well. Unlike other management methods that have caught the interest of business leaders—notably "excellence" in the 1980s, and "reengineering" in the 1990s—quality has proved to be a far richer and more durable idea. In fact, some observers have come to view quality as a basic management tool. In *Managing for the Future,* Gary Hamel and C. K. Pralahad argue that quality is no longer a competitive differentiator:

> In a recent survey, nearly 80 percent of U.S. managers polled believed that quality would be a fundamental source of competitive advantage in the year 2000. Yet, barely half of Japanese managers predicted quality to be a source of advantage in the year 2000, though 82 percent believed it was currently an important advantage. Rated first as a source of competitive advantage in the year 2000 by Japanese managers was a capacity to create fundamentally new products and businesses. Does this mean that Japanese managers are going to turn their backs on quality? Of course not. It merely indicates that by the year 2000 quality will no longer be a competitive differentiator; it will simply be the price of market entry.

Yet, these comments are based on an understanding of quality as *control* only, rather than as a larger concept that embraces both control and breakthrough, as Juran defines them. Highly-competitive organizations continue to turn to quality—in both senses of the word—to help them operate more efficiently *and* compete more successfully. For example, The General Electric Company (GE), one of the most profitable and successful companies in the United States, recently began a major quality program to help them, in chairman Jack Welch's words to "outperform the global business environment."

Although quality may no longer be considered the "hot" management discussion topic that it was in the 1980s, quality remains a central issue for our business organizations and our society. We are a long way from achieving quality in our manufactured products: aircraft still crash, air bags kill children, heart valves fail, copiers jam, computers fail, and pens leak. We are even further away from achieving quality in service businesses, from hospitality to videoconferencing. And then there are entire worlds of endeavor that scarcely have been touched by the quality process, including education, government, and the practice of law.

Juran refers to our current condition as "living behind the quality dikes." Although we receive wonderful benefits from technology, we also face substantial risks—from catastrophe to annoyance. "We are like the Dutch," he says. "They have taken advantage of technology to push the sea back and gain a lot of land, and all the advantages that presents. But it's a dangerous way to live because the sea isn't content to stay back. It wants to push back in." To hold back the sea, the Dutch rely on technology, in the form of dikes. Once built, the dikes must be maintained forever. "We're in the same situation when we adopt technology," says Juran. "We rely on quality—quality is our dike—to protect us from these annoyances and these terrible dangers."

Juran believes that all the chronic problems that we face today—environmental pollution, to governmental waste and inefficiency, to declining standards of education, to an overcomplicated, inequitable healthcare system—can be solved through quality management. We can gain control over any process, provoke breakthrough, and organize for continuous improvement. As Robert Galvin, former chairman of Motorola, likes to say, "Perfection *is* possible."

THE ROLE OF THE GURU

Today, the pursuit of quality—and of perfection—depends on the contribution of the outside expert: the consultant, the authority, the guru. Those who most deserve the appellation of "guru" tend to like it least—Deming refused to recognize it, Juran winces at it. Nevertheless, guru remains a widely used term for describing a special kind of contributor to the business scene. Although Peters defined the role of the business guru for the 1980s and after, the model has its roots in the consultants of the early twentieth century, including Gantt, Taylor, Gilbreth, and others.

The guru is:

- An independent practitioner, often an intellectual; a person with an organized and well-grounded body of knowledge, that contains original ideas or methods and information not to be found elsewhere.
- A teacher; a person with the ability to present knowledge in a way that is memorable and produces results.
- The guru generally is an author, preferably a best-selling one. The guru is almost always a speaker, who expands his or her influence through lectures and speeches, seminars and interviews.

However, these characteristics alone do not a full-fledged guru make. The guru may be an entertainer (Deming and Peters were, Juran was not), with the ability to arouse intense emotions in an audience. The

guru may be a consultant of the problem-solving variety, but that is a
perilous path to follow and the wise guru (all gurus should be wise)
does not promise to deliver any particular result. Finally, the guru, as
the name implies (the word, from the Hindustani language, means
teacher or priest), may have a religious aspect about him or her. That,
no doubt, is what most rankles the quality experts. Faith is the foundation of religion. Measurement is the foundation of quality. One cannot measure faith; faith is no substitute for a precise measurement. No
wonder that quality has taken deepest root in companies with engineering in their souls.

Juran prefers to call himself a "renaissance man" in the subject of
managing for quality; he might also be called an expert, an advocate,
or a master. Whatever it is called, the role of the independent expert
has become an increasingly important one since the early 1980s, essential to the smooth functioning of the business infrastructure. We
rely on the guru to accumulate knowledge through constant exposure
to a wide variety of ideas and practices, in many industries, organizations, and places. Business people cannot do this for themselves, because they are too busy running the business. And, besides, the
companies they most want to know about are their competitors, who
won't divulge secrets to anyone *but* a guru. We further expect the guru
to synthesize and distill all that accumulated knowledge, add some insightful analysis, infuse it all with wisdom, then package it and present
it to us in understandable and useful form. Business people cannot do
this either, because they lack the skills, the experience, and the opportunity. We also expect the guru to listen to us, hear what our ideas
and problems and solutions are, and incorporate them—if worthy—
into the guru's curriculum.

The role is tremendously useful; the business guru is the bee of
business who collects raw material (pollen) widely and converts it into
a far more valuable substance, the honey of understanding and advice
and wisdom. Unlike the bee, however, the guru does not reserve the
honey in a private inventory, but, instead, offers it for sale. The better the raw material, and the purer the distillation, the finer the product and the higher its price.

The guru role is also satisfying and rewarding to the practitioner. It provides the opportunity for constant learning through exposure to a steady stream of new people, ideas, information, practices, places, methods, processes, products, services, objects, machines, facilities, factories, situations, stories, anecdotes, bits of history, comments, conversations, jokes, and myths. Juran visited countless organizations, in some forty countries around the world. His guru role provided a platform for presenting and advocating cherished ideas, through writing, speaking, teaching, training, and being interviewed. Juran was constantly on the speaker circuit, and published widely. As a guru, he wielded great influence (his ideas were put into practice), and received much public recognition (awards, honorary doctorates, plaques, prizes), not to mention substantial financial gain. Juran consulted with government agencies, businesses, educational, and non-profit institutions. He received the prestigious Second Class Order of the Sacred Treasure from Emperor Hirohito of Japan, the National Medal of Technology from President George Bush, virtually every honor available from the quality organizations, and four honorary doctorate degrees. He made enough money to give the Institute he had founded to its employees, and to establish a charitable foundation.

One does not apply for a job as a business guru. Although gurus are needed, there are no positions available. The would-be guru must create the role for himself and convince the world that he or she can be trusted with the title. There are very few people who have sufficient experience, intelligence, knowledge, and will to be granted the job. Juran had all of those qualifications. What's more, he had a rare and visceral understanding of the role—an instinct, a *knack,* for it.

THE KNACK

Juran tells a story about a man named Knight, who worked in a foundry. The iron castings that Knight made were significantly better than those of his fellow workers. There were fewer defects, fewer rejects; Knight's castings met tolerances more closely than those of other workers. But no one in the foundry knew this, including Knight himself, because there were no markings on the castings to indicate which worker had made them, or when.

The managers of the foundry sought to improve their operations, to reduce defects, and improve quality. As a start, they analyzed their operations more closely than they ever had before. Part of the analysis involved scrutinizing the workers, tracing the finished parts to the person who had made them. To their great interest, they discovered the truth about Knight. They found that his work was far superior to the work of others, and they were curious to know why. What was this man doing differently and better than all the rest? Could whatever he was doing be emulated by the others? Could they use his techniques, match his output, and so improve the production of the foundry as a whole?

Then ensued a discussion among the managers about the best way to find out what Knight's secret was. The most obvious method, of course, was to go and talk with him. But, being managers in a traditionalist (Taylor-style) company, they were reluctant to so subordinate themselves to a line worker. It would look bad for a middle manager to seek knowledge from a lowly machine operator. Finally, sense and humanity prevailed, and they marched out of the executive offices and into the din of the foundry floor to interview the unsuspecting Knight.

Knight's secret was revealed almost immediately: he was an extremely tidy workman. He maintained his tools exceptionally well, always returning them to their proper place, keeping them in superior working order, and, above all, spotlessly clean. The cleanliness of Knight's tools prevented stray specks of dirt or foreign materials from contaminating the castings; the orderliness of their arrangement enabled Knight to work more swiftly and efficiently. The managers were deeply impressed. They instituted guidelines for the care and handling of tools which led to lower defect rates and better conformance to specifications throughout the foundry.

So absurdly simple.

Juran refers to the secret of the foundry worker as "the knack." Whether because of his nature, training, superior intelligence, or some other factor, Knight—without help from the system within which he worked—performed more successfully than his coworkers. And from that knack, others could learn and the whole organization could be improved. In his seventy years spent conferring in executive offices and visiting factory floors, Juran came across many instances of the knack. He found many people in a variety of activities who simply performed better than others, who thoroughly immersed themselves in their occupation, deeply learned about it, and became models.

Juran himself was one of those with the knack, if on a much broader scale than the foundry worker.

A Century's Crusade

Henry L. Gantt wrote of Frederick Taylor: "It was painful to him to see a group of people discussing a subject about which they were equally ignorant and deciding the question by vote. The great work of his life was a battle with such methods; the triumph of the scientific method over the debating society as a means of establishing a basis for action on questions involving the interest of employers and employees."

Juran's work can be seen as a battle similar to Taylor's: he strove to bring ratiocination, method, and measurement into the world of business. He called it quality and provided plenty of detail to define it, but it might as well be seen as an attitude. (He himself called it "quality-mindedness.") The attitude has, at its foundation, the scientific method: State a problem. Collect data. Form a hypothesis. Test it. Revise. Ad infinitum. But it is the scientific method applied to the practical pursuits of business, in which money, organization, and customers must be considered. The attitude has, as its arch enemy, what Taylor called "rule of thumb"—hunches, gut feelings, whims, faith, tradition, superstition, urges, wants. None of that should carry any weight in making business decisions and managing business activities.

Even in his boyhood jobs—as bookkeeper, package wrapper, newspaper boy—Juran found that he could go straight to the heart of the job, do it well, and as often as not, improve the way it was done— if his boss did not rebuff his ideas, as one of them did with a simple, "I don't pay you to think." In his first real job in business, as an inspector at Western Electric's Hawthorne Works, Juran soon demonstrated his knack but, here too, his desire to improve things ran into resistance. "That's not our job," his boss told him. "Our job is to inspect. The operations people run the factory." Juran never forgot the lesson—or antilesson. To this immigrant boy who had come to America with nothing, the idea of improvement was powerful.

Juran began his career with an expectation of staying at Western Electric and, eventually, of climbing the corporate ladder to some unspecified position near, or at, the top. Instead, he climbed only as high as the ranks of middle management, and then his way was blocked. He did not consider changing companies; he seems not to have considered seeking a position at Bell Labs or another research laboratory where a more collegial, intellectual atmosphere prevailed; he did some teaching at the university level, but didn't stick with it. He chose, instead, to become a professional outsider, an independent advocate for quality. In that role, he would address two audiences.

1. Technical people (engineers, manufacturers, inspectors, quality professionals). To them, he would provide a wealth of knowledge and tools with which to pursue quality. He would offer them the benefit of his years of experience, consideration, implementation, knowledge gathering, observation, analysis, and synthesis. He would also deliver to them a warning: If you want to be successful with quality in your organization, you will have to learn how to handle senior managers. And, believe me, you're not going to be able to get through to them by talking about control charts, statistics, and defect rates. You're going

to have to talk about the importance of quality to achieving business objectives and that means *money*.

2. Nontechnical managers, particularly senior executives. To them, he essentially said, *You must pay attention to quality!* You must personally get involved. You must train yourselves in its methods. You must devote considerable time and resource to getting everybody else in your organization involved. You can almost hear the message surging up from years of frustration with managers who wouldn't listen—from his first encounter with organizational barriers at Hawthorne to the blocking of his way at Western Electric's New York headquarters.

Over the years, Juran became more and more skilled in his ability to broaden the quality idea beyond its origins on the factory floor and extend it into the executive suite and, finally, into the entire organization. Then he helped to broaden the quality arena from manufacturing organizations to service companies and non-profit organizations and government agencies, and, finally, to society as a whole.

Although he was intent on delivering an urgent message to senior managers, his choice of communication channels and personal style did not always help him. For years, he delivered a course in general management in collaboration with the AMA, and the curriculum covered a broad range of management issues, not just those of quality. But it was a training course, not a discussion group, its audience was primarily composed of engineers and manufacturing personnel who were not yet managers, but wished to be. He may, therefore, have been speaking to *future* executives, but not directly to those in power.

His lectures and speaking engagements were most frequently to gatherings of engineers and quality professionals, particularly the various chapters of the ASQC. His writings generally appeared in such journals as *Mechanical Engineering* (published by the American Society of Mechanical Engineers), *Factory Management and Maintenance*, *Quality Progress* (the publication of the American Society for Quality Control), *Quality* magazine and *Personnel* magazine. Less often was his work published in management journals such as AMA's *Management Review.* Not until 1993 did a Juran article appear in *Harvard Business Review.*

In other words, Juran more often spoke to senior management *through* his engineering colleagues, rather than directly. At Gillette in the 1940s, and at other client companies, middle managers brought him in first (at one client, Bausch & Lomb, they virtually smuggled him in), and he eventually made his presentation to management. In Japan, the engineers of JUSE invited him to visit; they delivered the executives. At Rolls-Royce in the 1970s, and at Motorola in the 1980s, the pattern remained the same. In short, Juran's professional approach was, like his approach to quality, bottom-up.

All of this analysis helps to explain why Juran is less well-known than he deserves to be. Juran kept his nose to the grindstone. He was always working. When friends or family came to the house to visit, Juran would sit with them a while and then scurry back to his study and what he called "the world's work." He is extremely self-controlled, with rigorous habits and little time for chit-chat. His sense of humor is so understated as to be unnoticeable to many people, although delightfully dry in the opinion of others. There are precious few anecdotes about his actions or habits. People noticed that he walked fast; he said he got into the habit during the cold Minneapolis winters of his childhood. He demanded that twelve oranges be ready for him in his hotel room as a snack after delivering a lecture. He carried an inordinately small suitcase on extraordinarily long trips. He wore a black bow tie for most of his life.

Juran did not seek to become a guru. He did, however, successfully play out his chosen role as self-described "renaissance man of quality" and, in the process, helped to define and broaden the role played by independent advisers to business. Of all the roles he played—writer-teacher-consultant-speaker—the most important one may have been as teacher. He spent far more of his time training, teaching, and lecturing than he did on problem-solving assignments. His writings, too, have a didactic flavor; they are well-organized and amply supported with examples, and the citations are neatly noted. He is at his strongest when he gets to the how-to part.

As a result, Juran's ideas are more evident in our business organizations today than is his name. They include: his definition of quality; his sequences for achieving breakthrough and control; his understanding of the costs associated with quality; the Pareto Principle; the Juran Quality Trilogy—planning, control, improvement—that equates the language of quality with that of finance.

The consultancy business is one that, today, accommodates and depends on a variety of knacks. There are the evangelists. The problem solvers. The entertainers. The trainers. One of the most noble goals for a consultant is to put himself or herself out of business—to help clients learn something new and make it their own. Consultants, Juran leading among them, have long argued that any new initiative will only become effective if it becomes an essential part of the organizational culture. And that may be Juran's particular contribution—he has been so unprotective of his ideas, so willing to offer his services and energies, so unwilling to make a public fuss over credit, so ubiquitous and longevous, that his ideas have been thoroughly assimilated into good business practice. When Walter Shewhart died (in 1967), Juran wrote an appreciation of his former colleague that might be applied to himself. "At best (it seems to me) Shewhart's philosophical concepts have joined the numerous streams which collect and flow into our consciousness so thoroughly commingled that we cannot trace the sources."

Even as he approaches the century mark, Juran sees no end to his desire or ability to contribute to the great flow of ideas. "What I want to do has no end, since I am on the endless frontier of a branch of knowledge. I can go on as long as the years are granted to me. My job of contributing to the welfare of my fellow man is my great unfinished business now."

Notes

Chapter 1   A World without Quality

8   "... buzzed with flies in the summer and whistled up icy drafts in the winter": Nathan Juran, *Foot Loose in the World* (1992), p. 1.

Chapter 2   The Big Ship Hawthorne

21   "There were 46,000 people that worked at the Hawthorne plant, and I think that 43,000 of them had high heels. I did not get caught": Cecelia S. Killian, *The World of W. Edwards Deming* (2nd ed., Knoxville: SPC Press, 1992), p. 173.

22   "... the first period of hard times that the modern business enterprise had to face": Alfred Chandler, Jr., *The Visible Hand: The Managerial Revolution in American Business* (Cambridge: Belknap Press of Harvard University, 1977), p. 456.

23   "... as you could wish for if you liked that sort of thing": Alfred P. Sloan, Jr., *My Years with General Motors* (New York: Anchor Book Press, 1972), p. 45.

27   "'To my surprise,' wrote Juran, 'the result was only a slight drop in the defect rate'": Joseph M. Juran, "Renaissance In Quality" (Harvard Business Review, 1993).

29   "The inefficient rule-of-thumb methods, which are still almost universal in all trades, and in practicing which our workmen waste a large part of their effort": Frederick Winslow Taylor, *The Principles of Scientific Management* (1911, Reprint. New York: W. W. Norton, 1967), p. 16.

29   ". . . without the guidance and help of those who are working with him or over him, either through lack of education or through insufficient mental capacity": Ibid., p. 26.

30   "'. . . close, intimate, personal cooperation'—not a rigid, impersonal, authoritarian structure.": Ibid., pp. 25–26.

30   ". . . were simply interchangeable parts of the production system": James P. Womack, Daniel T. Jones, and Daniel Roos, *The Machine that Changed the World* (New York: Harper Perennial, 1990), p. 42.

31   ". . . to use full-time inspectors for product inspection and process control rather than to rely on the workmen": Joseph M. Juran, "The Taylor System and Quality Control," *Quality Progress* (May–December 1973), p. 15–30.

34   "The Bell System was now engaged in the manufacture of science, as well as telephones": Richard Gillespie, *Manufacturing Knowledge: A History of the Hawthorne Experiments* (Cambridge: Cambridge University Press, 1991), p. 28.

34   ". . . set forth all of the essential principles and considerations which are involved in what we know today as process quality control": William A. Golomski, "Walter A. Shewhart—Man of Quality—His Work, Our Challenge," *Industrial Quality Control* 24 (August 1967), p. 83.

34   ". . . random or chance fluctuation, i.e., not traceable to any specific cause": Joseph M. Juran, *Managerial Breakthrough: The Classic Book on Improving Management Performance* (2nd ed., New York: McGraw-Hill, 1995), p. 332.

35 "... non-assignable causes": W. A. Shewhart, "Quality Control Charts," *Bell System Technical Journal* (October 1926), p. 593.

35 "You try to make all the *a's* alike, but you don't; you can't. You are willing to accept this as an empirically established fact": Walter A. Shewhart, *Economic Control of Quality of Manufactured Product* (New York: D. Van Nostrand, 1931. Reprint. Milwaukee: ASQC Quality Press, 1980), p. 5.

36 "... which is no greater than that which could have resulted from the non-assignable causes": W. A. Shewhart, "Quality Control Charts," *Bell System Technical Journal* (October 1926), p. 594.

36 "Points outside the limit lines are almost certainly due to findable causes": Joseph M. Juran, *Managerial Breakthrough: The Classic Book on Improving Management Performance* (2nd ed., New York: McGraw-Hill, 1995), p. 332.

38 "... the image of a theorist, exhibiting some flashes of brilliance, but mainly impractical and unintelligible": "Tributes to Walter A. Shewhart," *Industrial Quality Control* (August 1967), p. 116.

39 "Through this re-examination, they challenged some defective premises": Joseph M. Juran, "Pioneering in Quality Control," *Industrial Quality Control* (September 1962), p. 13.

40 "In respect of hours of work and wages the Company stands above its compeers": Elton Mayo, *The Human Problems of an Industrial Civilization* (New York: The Macmillan Company, 1933. Reprint. Salem, New Hampshire: Ayer Company, 1992), p. 99.

41 "... their conditions of employment rapidly came to seem less and less bearable": James P. Womack, Daniel T. Jones, and Daniel Roos, *The Machine that Changed the World* (New York: Harper Perennial, 1990), p. 42.

41   "He had no apparent following, no apparent skills and less charm of manner": Ronald Pook, *Tales of Hawthorne: 1919–1947,* unpublished manuscript. (Location 44 11 01. Warren, NJ: AT&T Archives, 1988), p. 15.

42   ". . . the production of the control group increased about the same as that of the test group": Western Electric, *The Hawthorne Studies: A Synopsis, 1924/1974.* (Location 48 10 01. Warren, NJ: AT&T Archives, 1974), p. 2.

43   ". . . putting together a coil, armature, contact springs and insulators in a fixture and securing the parts in position by means of four machine screws": Elton Mayo, *The Human Problems of an Industrial Civilization* (New York: The Macmillan Company, 1933. Reprint. Salem, New Hampshire: Ayer Company, 1992), p. 57.

44   ". . . instead he came to be regarded as a friendly representative of management": F. J. Roethlisberger and William J. Dickson, *Management and the Worker* (Cambridge: Harvard University Press, 1939).

45   ". . . and exasperation in modern industry and business, although little can as yet be said of its occasion": Elton Mayo, *The Human Problems of an Industrial Civilization* (New York: The Macmillan Company, 1933. Reprint. Salem, New Hampshire: Ayer Company, 1992), p. 122.

Chapter 3   The $42-Billion Garden Hose

59   ". . . but Hopkins preferred to work from his bedroom on the second floor of the White House": Doris Kearns Goodwin, *No Ordinary Time* (1994) p. 214.

60   ". . . automobile wheels to gun mounts, from fireworks to ammunition, and from cotton mill machinery to howitzers for mountain fighting": Edward R. Stettinius, *Lend-Lease, Weapon for Victory* (New York: Macmillan Co., 1944), p. 100.

60 "Besides all the problems of production, there was the pressing problem of delivering the goods by sea and by air.": Ibid., p. 104.

60 "We must admit that the switch over from cash purchase to Lend-Lease has retarded the war effort by six months": George C. Herring, *An Experiment in Foreign Aid: Lend-Lease, 1941–1945* (PhD Dissertation, University of Virginia, 1965), p. 51.

60 "More than 1,200 uncleared requisitions were strewn around Hopkins' bedroom": Ibid., p. 51.

62 ". . . make provision for supplies, facilities and services": President of the United States, *Twentieth Report to Congress on Lend-Lease Operations, for the Period Ended June 30, 1945*, p. 65.

64 ". . . economy-minded oasis in a desert of empire-builders, proliferating payrolls, inefficiency and reckless spending": George C. Herring, *An Experiment in Foreign Aid: Lend-Lease, 1941–1945* (PhD Dissertation, University of Virginia, 1965), p. 161.

66 ". . . unheard-of opportunities for the bolder elements of the citizenry. Within a space of months some were holding down jobs which had been lifetime goals": Joseph M. Juran, *Bureaucracy: A Challenge to Better Management* (New York: Harper & Brothers, 1944), p. 18.

67 "Many tools of modern management are just waiting to be used": Ibid., p. 69.

Chapter 4   Launching the Canoe of Consultancy

75 ". . . installation of management methods": Ibid., p. 69.

78 ". . . the most important principles of application can be expounded in a very short time to engineers and others": W. Allen Wallis, "The Statistical Research Group, 1942–1945," *Journal of the American Statistical Association* 75 (June 1980), pp. 320–331.

79   ". . . the Second World War was won by quality control and by the utilization of modern statistics": Kaoru Ishikawa, *What Is Total Quality Control? The Japanese Way* (Translated by David J. Lu, Englewood Cliffs, NJ: Prentice Hall, Inc., 1985), p. 11.

80   "An elite corporal's guard of managers attended that pioneering event": Joseph M. Juran, "Management's Corner," *Industrial Quality Management* 11 (July 1964), p. 52.

80   "Not only could nothing stop it; nothing else could be heard above the roar": Ibid., p. 52.

83   ". . . in which all departments participate recurs again and again throughout the book": Paul C. Clifford, *Industrial Quality Control,* p. 104.

85   "Such a concept, is, however, too indefinite for practical purposes": Walter A. Shewhart, *Economic Control of Quality of Manufactured Product* (New York: D. Van Nostrand, 1931. Reprint. Milwaukee: ASQC Quality Press, 1980), p. 37.

85   ". . . in Latin *qualitas,* comes from *qualis,* meaning 'how constituted' and signifies such as the thing really is": Ibid., p. 38.

86   ". . . or any other requirement used to define the nature of a product or a service is a quality characteristic": Joseph M. Juran, *Quality Control Handbook* (1st ed., New York: McGraw-Hill, 1951), p. 2.

Chapter 5   Children of the Occupation

96   "One lone man with profound knowledge": Lloyd Dobyns and Clare Crawford-Mason, *Thinking About Quality: Progress, Wisdom, and the Deming Philosophy* (New York: Times Books, 1994), p. x.

96   ". . . for always providing an answer when asked an intriguing question": *Prophet Of Quality* video.

99   ". . . which had the most advanced communications technology in the world": Koji Kobayashi, "Quality Management at NEC Corporation," *Quality Progress* 19 (April 1986), p. 18.

100 "I remember that the yield of vacuum tubes for aircraft was one percent": Ibid., p. 18.

100 "NEC should practice quality control by all means, and that if I was interested he would help me": Ibid., p. 19.

100 "We first applied it to the production of vacuum tubes and we obtained remarkable results": Ibid., p. 19.

102 ". . . in shabby shacks where in a rainstorm, executives had to work with umbrellas over their desks": Kenneth Hopper, "Creating Japan's New Industrial Management: The Americans as Teachers," (Summer 1982), pp. 15–16.

103 ". . . 800,000 civilians had been killed or injured at home": Peter Duus, *The Rise of Modern Japan* (Boston: Houghton Mifflin Co., 1976), p. 238.

105 ". . . we should present a set of seminars on the principles of industrial management for top company executives": Kenneth Hopper, "Creating Japan's New Industrial Management: The Americans as Teachers" (Summer 1982), p. 19.

106 ". . . and also had it translated into a 488-page Japanese version": Joseph M. Juran, Editor, *A History of Managing for Quality: The Evolution, Trends, and Future Directions of Managing for Quality* (Milwaukee: ASQC Quality Press, 1995), p. 526.

107 ". . . some sheets of paper upon which are written some vague and inconclusive statements": Homer M. Sarasohn and Charles W. Protzman, *CCS: Industrial Management* (Cambridge: Harvard University, Baker Library, 1949), p. 90.

107 ". . . a multitude of different activities as is being demanded of these management people": Ibid., p. 93.

108 ". . . the course manual from 1950 cites L. P. Alford, a close colleague of Juran's at NYU, as a source": Kenneth Hopper, "Creating Japan's New Industrial Management: The Americans as Teachers" (Summer 1982), p. 20, note 16.

109 ". . . and its engineers made an important contribution to Japanese industry and the Japanese economy": Ibid., p. 29.

109 "It was not that we were not doing any of these things before, but it was good to get it all into a structured form": Joseph M. Juran, Editor, *A History of Managing for Quality: The Evolution, Trends, and Future Directions of Managing for Quality* (Milwaukee: ASQC Quality Press, 1995), p. 528.

109 ". . . we realized that what we had been doing was all wrong, and we were able to make dramatic progress": Ibid., p. 528.

111 ". . . ride his bicycle out in the country, come back minus the light bulbs but with rice and sake": Cecelia S. Killian, *The World of W. Edwards Deming* (2nd ed., Knoxville: SPC Press, 1992), p. 12.

111 ". . . because SCAP had to approve all newly forming Japanese organizations": Mary Walton, *The Deming Management Method* (New York: Perigee Books, 1986), p. 12.

111 ". . . and called for a 'united front in science and technology'": William M. Tsutsui, "W. Edwards Deming and the Origins of Quality Control in Japan" *Journal of Japanese Studies* 22 (Summer 1996), pp. 295–325.

111 ". . . but what it needed most desperately was modern scientific knowledge": Ibid.

112 ". . . in the case of quality control, or in anything that has the term 'control' attached to it, human and social factors are strongly at work": Kaoru Ishikawa, *What Is Total Quality Control? The Japanese Way* (Translated by David J. Lu, Englewood Cliffs, NJ: Prentice Hall, Inc., 1985), p. 16.

112 ". . . thought that a course by a famous statistician like Dr. Deming could bring about epochal results": Cecelia S. Killian, *The World of W. Edwards Deming* (2nd ed., Knoxville: SPC Press, 1992), p. 31.

113 "The list included thirteen names, including Shewhart, but not Juran": W. Edwards Deming, *The Elementary Principles of the Statistical Control of Quality, A Series of Lectures* (Tokyo: Nippon Kagaku Gijutsu Remmei, 1951), p. 5.

113 "In the same letter, we also asked if he could give a series of lectures on statistical quality control for several days while he was in Tokyo": Ibid., p. 5.

113 ". . . refusing an invitation from Ishikawa was about as sensible as refusing a request from Don Corleone": Jerry Bowles, "W. Edwards Deming: The Man and the Legend," *The Quality Executive* (January 1994).

113 ". . . as a member of an SCAP economic survey mission headed by Dr. A. S. Rice of Stanford University": Junji Noguchi, "The Legacy of W. Edwards Deming," *Quality Progress* 28 (December 1995), pp. 35–37.

115 ". . . new industrial age, created largely by statistical methods principles and techniques": W. Edwards Deming, *The Elementary Principles of the Statistical Control of Quality, A Series of Lectures* (2nd ed., Tokyo: Nippon Kagaku Gijutsu Remmei, 1951), p. 1.

115 ". . . it is necessary to carry out statistical tests and surveys": Ibid., p. 6.

118 ". . . the type he had studied at Ford's plants, 'could never work in Japan'": James P. Womack, Daniel T. Jones, and Daniel Roos, *The Machine that Changed the World* (New York: Harper Perennial, 1990), p. 48.

121 ". . . and that nothing would get better until they took personal responsibility for change": Jerry Bowles, "W. Edwards Deming: The Man and the Legend," *The Quality Executive* (January 1994).

121   "JUSE had charged each of the 440 attendees 15,000 yen (about
       $42)": Cecelia S. Killian, *The World of W. Edwards Deming* (2nd
       ed., Knoxville: SPC Press, 1992), p. 9.

121   ". . . although Noguchi claims the registration fee was only
       5,000 yen": Junji Noguchi, "The Legacy of W. Edwards Dem-
       ing," *Quality Progress* (December 1995), pp. 35–37. This ap-
       peared in a draft, but was omitted from the published version.

122   ". . . around $700 by 1960": William M. Tsutsui, "W. Edwards
       Deming and the Origins of Quality Control in Japan," *Journal
       of Japanese Studies* 22 (Summer 1996), pp. 295–325.

122   ". . . for any conscientious purpose": Cecelia S. Killian, *The
       World of W. Edwards Deming* (2nd ed., Knoxville: SPC Press,
       1992), p. 34.

122   "Television had not yet arrived, and radio offered a form of
       larger community and free entertainment": David Halberstam,
       The Reckoning (New York: William Morrow and Co., 1986),
       p. 302.

122   ". . . many Japanese observers were discouraged to find that
       Deming had no new tricks to pull from his statistical hat":
       M. William Tsutsui, "W. Edwards Deming and the Origins of
       Quality Control in Japan," *Journal of Japanese Studies* 22 (Sum-
       mer 1996), pp. 295–325.

124   "Japan's exports will have to be increased by a minimum of 40
       percent": Sgigeto Tsuru, "A New Japan? Political, Economic,
       and Social Aspects of Postwar Japan." *Atlantic Monthly* 195 (Jan-
       uary 1955), p. 106.

125   "What Japan requires most of all over the long term is foreign
       markets in which she can sell at a reasonable profit the products
       of the export industry": Arthur H. Dean, "Japan at the Cross-
       roads," *The Atlantic Monthly* 194 (November 1954), p. 34.

125   "I faced an audience of 70 leading CEOs, but that was for one
       hour": Joseph M. Juran, *Harvard Business Review,* p. 2.

126   "That's why the people in Japan consider Dr. Deming an easy person to get along with": Junji Noguchi, "The Legacy of W. Edwards Deming," *Quality Progress* 28 (December 1995), p. 9.

126   "In that way, Dr. Juran gave the Japanese presidents very good lessons": Interview with Hajime Karatsu by Howland Blackiston and Jack Schatz, March 18, 1992, Tokyo, Japan.

127   "My hosts explained to me the implications of the Japanese concept of mutual lifelong responsibilities between worker and company": "The Japanese Revolution in Quality—Remembrance and Prognosis," *Quality Progress* 9 (February 1976), pp. 8–10.

130   ". . . with his thoughts on how managers should take charge of quality and what their role should be": Joseph M. Juran, *Harvard Business Review.*

131   "Juran's inspiration was like a 'welcome rain' to JUSE's parched and wilting quality crusade": M. William Tsutsui, "W. Edwards Deming and the Origins of Quality Control in Japan," *Journal of Japanese Studies* 22 (Summer 1996), pp. 295–325.

132   "And around those programs the Japanese built a quality revolution": Joseph M. Juran, *Harvard Business Review.*

132   "He had said that quality should be their top priority, and that quality came even before profit": Andrea Gabor, *The Man Who Discovered Quality: How W. Edwards Deming Brought the Quality Revolution to America—The Stories of Ford, Xerox, and GM* (New York: Penguin Books, 1992), p. 87.

133   ". . . participated by all employees of an organization, is based on Dr. Juran's lessons": Junji Noguchi, "The Legacy of W. Edwards Deming." *Quality Progress* 28 (December 1995), p. 10.

133   ". . . masterful teaching gave to Japanese management new insight into management's responsibility for improvement of quality and productivity": W. Edwards Deming, *Out of the*

Crisis (Cambridge: M.I.T. Center for Advanced Engineering Study, 1982), p. 489.

133 "The cooperation of the people working at the same work place is the basis for everything": Junji Noguchi, "The Legacy of W. Edwards Deming," *Quality Progress* 28 (December 1995), pp. 35–37.

Chapter 6   Breakthrough and Bliss

139 "If he receives an invitation to lecture abroad, there is no need to ask the bureaucracy if he may go. He just goes": Joseph M. Juran, "So you want to be a Quality Consultant," *Quality Progress* 23 (December 1966), pp. 265–270.

140 ". . . restated in a more generalized, orderly form": Joseph M. Juran, *Managerial Breakthrough: The Classic Book on Improving Management Performance* (2nd ed., New York: McGraw-Hill, 1995), pp. 12–13.

140 "Managers are busy doing both of these things, and nothing else": Ibid., p. 5.

141 "Failing in this, the company ages, decays, and dies": Ibid., p. 4.

142 "A supervisor vows 'We'll fix this thing once and for all'": Ibid., p. 21.

144 "In contrast, our effort, if applied solely to the trivial many, is always a failure": Joseph M. Juran, *Managerial Breakthrough: The Classic Book on Improving Management Performance* (2nd ed., New York: McGraw-Hill, 1995), p. 21.

145 "Lorenz offered a graphical method of showing the distribution of wealth": M. O. Lorenz, "Methods of Measuring the Concentration of Wealth," *American Statistical Association* 9 (June 1905), pp. 209–219.

145 ". . . and I had no qualms about Pareto's name. Hence the Pareto Principle": Joseph M. Juran, "The Non-Pareto Principle: Mea Culpa," *Quality Progress* 8 (May 1975), pp. 2–15.

147 "In the factory she is asked to adjust her rhythm to that of the rhythm prescribed by the factory; to do things according to externally set time limits": Margaret Mead, Editor, *Cultural Patterns and Technical Change* (Deventer, Holland: UNESCO, 1953), p. 257.

148 ". . . when a financial adviser from the United States discovered that it was the pattern in government offices": Ibid., p. 262.

Chapter 7   The Desperate Decade

154 ". . . as well as to broaden the extent of worker participation in the affairs of the company": Joseph M. Juran, *Juran on Quality by Design: The New Steps for Planning Quality into Goods and Services* (New York: Free Press, 1992), p. 395.

159 ". . . had sold a total of some 17,000 books": Joseph M. Juran, "Then and Now in Quality Control: And One Makes Fifty," *Quality Progress* 8 (March 1975), pp. 4–5.

163 ". . . the turning point between academic obscurity and public fame": Lloyd Dobyns and Clare Crawford-Mason, *Thinking About Quality: Progress, Wisdom, and the Deming Philosophy* (New York: Times Books, 1994), p. ix.

164 "Our phones rang off the hook. Dr. Deming's mail quadrupled, and beyond": Cecelia S. Killian, *The World of W. Edwards Deming* (2nd ed., Knoxville: SPC Press, 1992), p. 255.

165 "They offered to purchase an equity position in our company in order to make things more permanent": Philip Crosby, *Quality Is Still Free: Making Quality Certain in Uncertain Time* (New York: McGraw-Hill, 1996), p. 155.

166 ". . . a standard that management can convey to the employees to help them to decide to 'do the job right the first time' ": Philip B. Crosby, *Quality Is Free: The Art of Making Quality Certain* (New York: Mentor, 1980), p. 145.

167   "This conclusion had little relation to reality; however, the program was cleverly presented and was persuasive to many viewers": Joseph M. Juran, "World War II and the Quality Movement," *Quality Progress* (December 1991), p. 24.

168   "There is good news from America. Good management practice today is not resident only in Japan": Thomas J. Peters and Robert H. Waterman, Jr., *In Search of Excellence: Lessons from America's Best-Run Companies* (New York: Warner Books, 1982), p. xxiii.

168   ". . . to an America that was worried about its declining competitiveness but tired of being told about the Japanese miracle": John Micklethwait and Adrian Wooldridge, *The Witch Doctors: Making Sense of the Management Gurus* (New York: Times Books, 1996), p. 82.

169   "What is wrong with us? And what are we doing to remedy it?": Frank Gibney, *Miracle by Design: The Real Reasons Behind Japan's Economic Success* (New York: Times Books, 1982), p. 4.

169   "The United States may be today the most under-developed nation in the world": W. Edwards Deming, *Out of the Crisis* (Cambridge: M.I.T. Center for Advanced Engineering Study, 1982), p. 6.

169   ". . . and she gives him *In Search of Excellence* you know that management has become part of the general culture": John Micklethwait and Adrian Wooldridge, *The Witch Doctors: Making Sense of the Management Gurus* (New York: Times Books, 1996), p. 83.

171   "There is no true value of the speed of light; no true value of the number of inhabitants within the boundaries of (e.g.) Detroit": Walter A. Shewhart, *Statistical Method from the Viewpoint of Quality Control.* Edited by W. Edwards Deming (Washington, DC: Graduate School of the Department of

Agriculture, 1939. Reprint with new foreword by W. Edwards Deming. New York: Dover Publications, 1986), p. i.

171 ". . . the concept underlying the quality control chart technique of 1924 was born of a probable science": Ibid., p. 4.

172 "Unless this mine is demonstrably large enough to pay for the cost of digging, there will very likely be no digging": Joseph M. Juran, *Quality Control Handbook* (1st ed., New York: McGraw-Hill, 1951), p. 180.

Chapter 8   Guru at the Dikes

183 "It merely indicates that by the year 2000 quality will no longer be a competitive differentiator; it will simply be the price of market entry": Gary Hamel and C. K. Prahalad, *Competing for the Future* (Boston: Harvard Business School Press, 1994), p. 15.

184 ". . . outperform the global business environment": *Wall Street Journal* (January 13, 1997), p. 1.

189 ". . . establishing a basis for action on questions involving the interest of employers and employees": Henry Gantt, *Gantt on Management: Guidelines for Today's Executive,* Edited by Alex W. Rathe (New York: American Management Association, The American Society of Engineers, 1961), p. 39.

193 ". . . which collect and flow into our consciousness so thoroughly commingled that we cannot trace the sources": "Tributes to Walter A. Shewhart," *Industrial Quality Control* (August 1967), p. 116.

Chronology of Key Dates

Dates related to Juran appear in roman text.
Dates related to the development of the quality movement appear in italics.

1846

Frederick W. Taylor born.

1848

Vilfredo Pareto born.

1860s

Grandfather arrives in Gurahumora, Romania.

1874

May 20, Jakob Juran (father) born.

1880

April 15, Gitel Goldenburg (mother) born.

1886

Arthur D. Little founds consulting firm, ADL.

1891

March 18, Walter A. Shewhart born.

1900

circa: Jakob Juran moves to Braila from Gurahumora.
W. Edwards Deming born in Iowa.

1901

Henry L. Gantt becomes consulting engineer.

1902

Brother Rudy born.
AT&T expansion begins.

1903

Sister Rebecca born.
AT&T purchases land to build Hawthorne plant in Chicago.

1904

December 24, Joseph Juran born in Braila, Romania.
Hawthorne Works construction begins.

1905

March, Sadie Shapiro (wife) born.
Hawthorne plant completed.
Lorenz publishes article in Journal of the American Statistical Association *re Pareto curve.*

1906

Jurans move from Braila back to Gurahumora.

1907

Brother Nathan (nicknames: Nat, Jerry) born.

Frank Gilbreth founds Taylor Society.

AT&T centralizes all research and engineering at Hawthorne Works.

Arthur Andersen founds Andersen, DeLany & Co., Chicago.

1909

Jakob arrives in Minneapolis. Lives with Kliffer family.

1910

Jakob moves (with Herman Kliffer) to 514 Twelfth Avenue South.

Western Electric begins recruiting at colleges.

1911

Joe attends public school in Gurahumora.

Jakob boards at Isaac Sullivan home, 712 Oak Lake Avenue.

1912

August, the rest of the Juran family leaves Europe through the port of Antwerp, Belgium.

August 19, ship *Mount Temple* docks in Quebec.

August 22, they enter United States. Take up residence at 3445 Central Avenue Northwest, Minneapolis.

Joe begins schooling at the Prescott School.

April 12, Titanic sinks.

1913

Sister Minerva born.

Joe works as a newsboy, selling the *Tribune* in the morning and the *Journal* in the afternoon; as a bootblack roving the streets, offering a shoeshine for 5 cents; as grocery clerk at O.J. Walker's.

Henry Ford employs assembly line for manufacture of complete automobile at Highland Park plant of Ford Motor Company.

1914

World War I begins in Europe.

1915

Joe works at Peter Corbin's icehouse as bookkeeper.

Summer, drives Corbin's sprinkler wagon, to keep dust down in the streets.

Sister Charlotte born.

Frederick W. Taylor dies.

Telephone wires stretch coast to coast.

1916

Joe works as a packer at Boutelle Brothers.

Attends East High School, between University Avenue and Fourth Street.

1917

Family moves to 2916 East 25th Street, Minneapolis, replete with indoor plumbing and toilets.

Joe becomes a U.S. citizen.

Works on the staff of the *Southerner,* the school newspaper, at South High School.

Member of the Technical Club; visits manufacturing plants in the Twin Cities and completes a wireless set.

Works as an errand boy for State Prohibition Commission.

Works as an office boy for W. G. Calderwood.

United States enter World War I.

1918

Joe works as a shipping clerk for Root Hageman.

Family moves to new house.

World War I ends.

AT&T decides to make automated telephone exchanges.

Walter A. Shewhart joins AT&T.

1919

Joe works as a bundle boy and a shoe salesman for M. W. Savage.

Family fortunes improve, thanks to Jakob's bootlegging.

1920

May, Gitel (mother) enters Hopewell Hospital.

June, Joe graduates from high school in the June Division as one of 20 honor students from a class of 226.

Works as a house wrecker for M. J. Rose.

Works as a printer's helper for Standard Press and others.

September 4, Gitel, dies at age 40. Is buried in the Minneapolis Jewish Cemetery at 70½ Penn Avenue South in Richfield.

Two younger sisters are placed in orphanage.

Joe moves with Jakob and brother Nat to a duplex at 2823 Grand Avenue South.

Jakob operates a shoe repair shop at 110 Second Avenue.

Fall, Joe enters the University of Minnesota as electrical engineering student.

U.S. in recession.

Eugene V. Debs runs for President.

Western Electric begins advertising for recruits at colleges.

Warren G. Harding elected President.

1921

Joe works as a draftsman.

Takes chess championship at University of Minnesota.

1922

Joe works as electrician's helper for C.B.&Q. Railroad; as a shipping clerk for M. J. Rosenstein; as a shoe salesman for Kinney's.

Wallace Clark publishes The Gantt Chart: A Working Tool of Management.

G. S. Radford publishes The Control of Quality in Manufacturing.

Time Standards Department established at Hawthorne.

Vilfredo Pareto dies.

AT&T introduces centralized switching device.

1923

Joe works as chess editor for *Minneapolis Daily Star,* and as a shipping clerk for Heinz Medical Institute.

Joe joins ROTC, Signal Reserve.

President Harding dies.

1924

June, Joe graduates from University of Minnesota with BS in Electrical Engineering.

Receives three job offers.

Moves to Chicago.

June, starts at Hawthorne Works. Assigned to Inspection Branch.

Meets Sadie Shapiro at train station.

American Management Association (AMA) founded.

May, Shewhart proposes his control chart to George Edwards.

Elton Mayo (from Harvard) begins his experiments at Western Electric.

Calvin Coolidge elected President.

1925

Joe rooms with Ray Egli and his wife, in a ground floor of a duplex on Kostner Street.

February, becomes investigator in shop complaint department.

June 26, marries Sadie Shapiro. Sadie's mother moves in with them.

Joe is commissioned into Signal Reserve.

Summer, Deming works at Hawthorne on transmitters.

Edwin Booz founds firm in Chicago.

Western Electric engineering department spins off Bell Laboratories.

12 million phones in U.S.

Bell Labs creates first recognizable TV picture (Picturephone).

1926

Joe begins to work for C. A. Malsheimer. Responsibility: "Application of theory of possibilities for Inspection practices—sampling, quality control, etc."

Begins to apply SQC to manufacturing.

Summer, Deming works at Hawthorne.

James McKinsey, accounting professor at University of Chicago, founds McKinsey & Company, Chicago.

Severe industrial strikes in Japan.

Scientists from Bell Labs study production at Western Electric.

First telephone conversation across the Atlantic.

1927

January, son Robert is born.

Deming joins the Department of Agriculture. He meets Shewhart.

Spring, Elton Mayo conducts his experiments at Hawthorne.

1928

Juran writes pamphlet, *Statistical Methods Applied to Manufacturing Problems.*

Designs training course at Hawthorne.

Mayo experiments are expanded to interview 20,000 employees.

1929

Promoted to "Supervisor of engineers doing Inspection staff work involving time study, job evaluation, wage determination, budgeting, application of theory of probabilities to inspection practices, quality audits." Reports to: G. L. Schnable.

1930

January, daughter Sylvia born.

1931

January 2, father dies of a heart attack while playing pinochle. Is buried in the same cemetery as Gitel, although not next to her.

Promotion. Supervises "engineers engaged in investigation of shop difficulties, customers' quality complaints and disposition of defective products. Also supervision of time study, job evaluation, and wage determination work."

Begins attending Loyola University to study law.

Son Chuck born.

Walter Shewhart publishes Economic Control of Quality of Manufactured Product.

1932

Worst year of the Depression. Layoffs at Hawthorne Works.

1933

In Chicago, 50 percent of the workforce is unemployed.

1934

Promotion. Supervises "inspection of purchased materials and of electrical laboratory."

Hawthorne experiments end.

Industrial boom period in Japan, through 1936.

1935

January, Joe receives a JD degree from Loyola University.

First of U.S. Neutrality Acts passed.

1936

Becomes a member of the Illinois Bar.

Begins taking accounting classes at Northwestern University.

1937

Promoted to head of Industrial Engineering Department. Responsibilities: Job evaluation, time study, wage determination, salary determination, and wage policy questions generally for all factories of the Western Electric Co.

Moves to corporate headquarters at 195 Broadway, New York.

November 26, moves family to 4 Watchung Place, Summit, NJ.

Articulates Pareto Principle.

Shewhart, at the invitation of Deming, gives four lectures on statistical method from the viewpoint of quality control at the Graduate School of the Department of Agriculture, Washington, DC.

1939

Shewhart publishes Statistical Method from the Viewpoint of Quality Control.

Deming develops sampling methods for the U.S. Census.

Deming leaves Department of Agriculture.

1940

June, France signs armistice with Germany.

1941

March, son Don born.

December 25, Juran asked to serve temporarily as Assistant Administrator for the Lend-Lease Program in the Foreign Economic Administration.

March 11, Office of Lend-Lease Administration (OLLA) established.

December 7, Pearl Harbor attacked. U.S. enters World War II.

1942

May, cross-functional team at OLLA begins to meet.

Summer, family moves to Arlington, Virginia.

October, the committee makes its report.

Deming advises on Statistical Quality Control at War Production Board seminars.

1943

Joe helps prepare report on OLLA activities to Congress.

Begins to plan his new career.

Workload eases.

War Production Board sponsors the famous eight-day courses in quality control, through 1945.

Edward Stettinius leaves OLLA to become Undersecretary of State under President Franklin D. Roosevelt.

1944

Publishes *Bureaucracy: A Challenge to Better Management.*

1945

July 3, resigns from Western Electric.

September 1, leaves OLLA. Serves as professor and chairman of Department of Industrial Engineering at NYU.

Publishes *Management of Inspection and Quality Control.*

Receives Worcester Reed Warner Medal, from American Society of Mechanical Engineers (ASME).

August, Lend-Lease ends.

World War II ends.

Occupation of Japan begins.

1946

Consults with Gillette.

Japanese Union of Scientists and Engineers (JUSE) forms Quality Control Research Group.

Deming joins NYU as professor at Graduate School of Business Administration.

American Society for Quality Control (ASQC) is founded.

Magil departs Japan.

Homer Sarasohn arrives in Japan.

1947

Deming invited to Japan by Supreme Command for the Allied Powers (SCAP) to help on the 1950 census.

1948

Juran lectures at Sweden's Royal Institute of Technology.

Drucker advises GM to get into quality.

Lawrence Appley becomes president of American Management Association (AMA).

1949

Teaches course at NYU: "Management of Inspection and Quality Control."

Creates course on "Managing for Quality" through AMA.

Polkinghorn arrives in Japan.

September 26–November 18. First Civil Communication Section (CCS) seminar conducted at Waseda University, Tokyo.

1950

Quits NYU.

January, second round of CSS seminars.

Summer, Deming lectures in Japan.

1951

Quality Control Handbook published by McGraw-Hill.

First Deming Prizes awarded in Japan.

1952

Juran is invited to visit Japan by Kobayashi, at ASQC meeting in New York.

American occupation of Japan ends.

1953

Juran visits Australia and conducts series of lectures.

1954

July–August, Juran delivers lectures in Japan.

Receives Alumni Medal, University of Minnesota.

1955

Publishes (with N. N. Barish) *Case Studies in Industrial Management.*

Japanese GNP reaches prewar levels.

1956

Begins editing "Management Corner" column in *Quality Progress* magazine.

Publishes *Lectures in Quality Control* (in Japanese).

1958

Receives Brumbaugh Award from ASQC.

1960

Publishes *Lectures in General Management* (in Japanese).

Returns to Japan.

Deming awarded the Second Class Order of the Sacred Treasure by Japan.

1961

Receives Edwards Medal from ASQC.

Receives Scroll of Appreciation from JUSE.

1962

Second edition, *Quality Control Handbook* published.

1964

Publishes *Managerial Breakthrough*.

Olympic Games held in Tokyo.

1965

Receives 250th Anniversary Medal, Czechoslovakian Higher Institute of Technology.

1966

Tells an audience in Stockholm that Japanese will achieve world leadership in quality within two decades.

Publishes (with J. Keith Louden) *The Corporate Director*.

1967

Receives Wallace Clark Medal from ASME and AMA.

Publishes "The QC Circle Phenomenon" in *Industrial Quality Control* magazine.

1968

Receives Medal of Technikhaza, Esztergom, Hungary.

Named Honorary Member of ASQC. One of just 14 people so honored, since the founding of ASQC.

1970

Receives Medal of Honor Camera Official de la Industria, Madrid.

Publishes *Quality Planning and Analysis* (with Frank M. Gryna).

1973

Publishes *The Taylor System and Quality Control,* a series of articles in "Quality Progress" magazine.

1974

Third edition of *Quality Control Handbook* published.

Lillian Gilbreth dies.

End of CCS seminars in Japan.

1975

Juran estimates that Japan draws even with the United States on quality.

1976

Addresses Institute of Quality Assurance at Imperial College, London University.

1979

Founds the Juran Institute. Serves as Chairman. Creates and markets *Juran on Quality Improvement* videos.

Publishes "Japanese and Western Quality—A Contrast," in *Quality* magazine.

1980

Estimates that Japan is ahead of the United States on quality.

Philip Crosby publishes Quality is Free.

June 24, 9:30 P.M. "If Japan can . . . Why Can't We" broadcast on NBC.

1981

Receives the Second Class Order of the Sacred Treasure from Emperor Hirohito.

Receives Gilbreth Award, American Institute of Industrial Engineers.

1982

In Search of Excellence *published by Tom Peters.*

1983

Inducted to AMA Wall of Fame.

1984

Receives Stevens Medal, Stevens Institute of Technology.

Kansei Electric wins Deming Prize, the first service company to do so.

1986

Founds the Juran Foundation and serves as Chairman.

Visits Romania at invitation of Romanian government.

Testifies before Congress *re* establishment of Malcolm Baldrige National Quality Award.

Begins four-year service on the Baldrige Board of Overseers.

Malcolm Baldrige National Quality Award established.
Chernobyl disaster in USSR.

1987

Becomes Chairman Emeritus of the Juran Institute. A. Blanton Godfrey named chairman.

1988

Receives Chairman's Award, American Association of Engineering
Societies.
Fourth edition of *Quality Control Handbook* is published.
Publishes *Juran on Planning for Quality.*

1989

Publishes *Juran on Leadership for Quality: An Executive Handbook.*

1992

Receives National Medal of Technology for Technology Management
in ceremony with President George Bush. Cited for "development of
key principles and methods by which enterprises manage the quality
of their products and processes."
Publishes *Juran on Quality by Design.*

1993

Third edition of *Quality Planning and Analysis* published.
Last Word Tour begins.
Publishes article in *Harvard Business Review,* *re* role in Japan.

1995

Publishes *A History of Managing for Quality.*

Acknowledgments

D
r. Juran cooperated in the writing of this book, the first time he has agreed to "authorize" a biography about him. His participation was limited, however, because of the urgency of his own writing—he is producing a five volume autobiography and, at age 92, intensely feels the pressure of time. He granted two long interviews, as well as access to some materials and personal papers.

We were given access to many other of Dr. Juran's papers, as well as the transcripts of several additional interviews with him (see bibliography), as part of our involvement with the writing of the television documentary, *An Immigrant's Gift*. The program chronicles the life of Dr. Juran, and began airing on many Public Broadcasting System stations in December 1996.

We are grateful to G. Howland Blackiston, President of Juran Institute (and of Woodsend Productions, producers of the documentary), for his help, cooperation, guidance, and insight throughout the project and for the use of the interviews with Juran's colleagues and family members conducted for *An Immigrant's Gift*. We also appreciate the insight and help of A. Blanton Godfrey, Chairman of the Institute, and Laura Sutherland, Dr. Juran's personal secretary.

I was aided in the research and writing of the book by my associates, John De Lancey and Russell Lynde. John acted as chief researcher, with particular responsibility for the sections on Hawthorne, postwar

Japan, and Gillette; Russell had responsibility for the section on Lend-Lease, as well as other assignments.

Thanks to Kenneth Hopper for his interest in the book and help in providing information and insight about the activities of CCS staff members during the period 1946–1950. Larry Frey, of the Minnesota section of the ASQC, provided much detail on Juran's early life in Minneapolis, and welcome insights on the manuscript. Rick Wheeler, who spent several years in Japan, was informative and helpful in many ways.

Sincere thanks to those who reviewed the manuscript and offered their comments, corrections, and insights: Robert J. Ballon, Robert Butman, Clare Crawford-Mason, Armand V. Feigenbaum, Frank Gryna, Jane Roessner, Homer Sarasohn, Leonard Seder, Meyer Shnitzler, Brad Stratton, Myron Tribus, and Glenn Williams.

Thanks to my editor at John Wiley & Sons, Jeanne Glasser, who was supportive and effective throughout the writing process, and to Myles Thompson, publisher, who helped initiate the project.

Thanks, finally, to my family, Nancy, Jeremy, and Henry, for their love and support.

Bibliography

JOSEPH M. JURAN

Articles

"Inspectors' Errors in Quality Control." *Mechanical Engineering* 57 (October 1935): 643–644.

"The A,B,C of Quality Control." *Mechanical Engineering* 66 (August 1944): 529–535.

"The Relation of the Quality Function to the Industrial Enterprise." *Industrial Quality Control* 3 (July 1946): 5–7.

and R. E. Wareham. "Progress in Quality Control." In *8th International Management Congress,* Vol. 1, 467–474. Stockholm: Esselte Aktiebolag, 1947.

"Transition in Corporate Controls." *Advanced Management* 8 (September 1948): 126–130.

"Application of Statistics to the Science of Management." *Mechanical Engineering* 71 (April 1949): 321–324.

Review of *Frank and Lillian Gilbreth,* by Edna Yost. *Mechanical Engineering* 71 (July 1949): 610–611.

"Insure Success for Your Quality Control Program." *Factory Management and Maintenance* 108 (October 1950): 106–109.

"Management Techniques for Stimulating Productivity." In *Industrial Productivity: A Social and Economic Analysis,* edited by Industrial Relations Research Association. (Madison, WI: Industrial Relations Research Association, 1951): 76–93.

"Can Your Processes Hold the Tolerances You've Set?" *Factory Management and Maintenance* 110 (June 1952): 118–120.

"Directions for ASQC." *Industrial Quality Control* 8 (November 1951): 30–34.

"Is Your Product Too Fussy?" *Factory Management and Maintenance* 110 (August 1952): 125–128.

"Installing a Quality Control System." *Industrial Quality Control* 7 (May 1953): 21–22.

"Nine Steps to Better Quality." *Factory Management and Maintenance* 112 (March 1954): 106–108.

"Management's Corner." *Industrial Quality Management* 11 (July 1954): 54.

"The Anatomy of Industrial Habits." In *Adjusting to a Competitive Economy—the Human Problem* (American Management Association, Manufacturing Series No. 214, 1954): 34–47.

"Universals in Management Planning and Controlling." *The Management Review* 43 (November 1954): 748–761.

"Production Planning and Control as an Interdivisional Responsibility." In *Successful Production Planning and Control: From Forecast to Final Delivery* (American Management Association, Special Report No. 5, 1955): 27–33.

"The Top Executive's Responsibilities for Quality." *Industrial Quality Control* 11 (May 1955): 34–38.

"Management's Corner: Dealing with the 'Obstructionist' Superintendent." *Industrial Quality Control* 12 (July 1955): 24.

"Improving the Relationship Between Staff and Line: An Assist From the Anthropologists." *Personnel* 32 (May 1956): 515–524.

"Management's Corner: Progress for QC Engineers—Horizontal or Vertical?" *Industrial Quality Control* 12 (May 1956): 108–110.

"Industrial Diagnostics." *The Management Review* 46 (June 1957): 79–91.

"Industrial Engineering and the Challenge of Modern Manufacturing Problems." In *Line-Staff Relationships in Production* (American Management Association, Special Report No. 18, 1957): 113–117.

"Cultural Patterns and Quality Control." *Industrial Quality Control* 14 (October 1957): 8–13.

"Identifying and Solving the Company's Major Quality Problems." In *Quality Control in Action: Tools, Techniques, and Administrative Guides* (American Management Association, Management Report No. 9, 1958): 27–32.

"Pareto, Lorenz, Cournot, Bernoulli, Juran and Others." *Industrial Quality Control* 17 (October 1960): 25.

"Japan Revisited." *Industrial Quality Control* 17 (March 1961): 32.

"A Visit to Complex Systems, Inc." *Industrial Quality Control* 18 (January 1962): 37–40.

"Pioneering in Quality Control." *Industrial Quality Control* 19 (September 1962): 12–14.

"Different to You But Alike to Me." *Industrial Quality Control* 19 (April 1963): 32–33.

"Seminars for QC Management—At Last." *Industrial Quality Control* 21 (July 1964): 52.

"The Two Worlds of Quality Control." *Industrial Quality Control* 21 (November 1964): 238–244.

"Whose Quality Costs?" *Industrial Quality Control* 22 (August 1965): 82–83.

"Quality Problems, Remedies, and Nostrums." *Industrial Quality Control* 22 (June 1966): 647–653.

"So You Want to Be a Quality Consultant." *Industrial Quality Control* (December 1966): 265–270.

"The Japanese QC Circles: Questions and Answers." *Quality* (No. 2, 1967): 37–38.

"The QC Circle Phenomenon." *Industrial Quality Control* 23 (January 1967): 329–336.

"Tribute to Walter Shewhart." *Industrial Quality Control* 24 (August 1967) 116.

"Operator Errors—Time for a New Look." *Quality Progress* 1 (February 1968): 9–11, 54.

"Mobilizing for the 1970's." *Quality Progress* 2 (August 1969): 8–17.

"Consumerism and Product Quality." *Quality Progress* 3 (July 1970): 18–27.

"Quality Control in Service Industries." *Quality* 3 (1973). Reprint.

"The Taylor System and Quality Control." Parts 1–8. *Quality Progress* 6 (May–December 1973): 42, 33, 41, 33, 26, 36, 31.

"Then and Now in Quality Control: And One Makes Fifty." *Quality Progress* 8 (March 1975): 4–5.

"Quality Control of Service—The 1974 Japanese Symposium." *Quality Progress* 8 (April 1975): 10–13.

"The Non-Pareto Principle: Mea Culpa." *Quality Progress* 8 (May 1975): 2–15.

"Khruschev's Venture into Quality Improvement." *Quality Progress* 9 (January 1976): 4.

"The Japanese Revolution in Quality—Remembrance and Prognosis." *Quality Progress* 9 (February 1976): 8–10.

"That Uninterested Top Management." *Quality Progress* 10 (December 1977): 18–19.

"Japanese and Western Quality—A Contrast." Parts 1, 2. *Quality* (January/February 1979): 8–12, 12–15.

"Product Quality—A Prescription for the West." Parts 1, 2. *The Management Review* 71 (June/July 1981): 18–24, 57–61.

"Charting the Quality Course." Presented at the 29th Conference of the European Organization for Quality Control, at Estoril, Portugal, June 1985.

"The Quality Trilogy: A Universal Approach to Managing Quality." *Quality Progress* 19 (August 1986): 19–24.

"A Tale of the Twentieth Century." *The Juran Report* 10 (1989): 4–13.

"Joseph Juran Plans the Future." An interview with Stephen McClelland. *Total Quality Management* (November 1989): 271–274.

"Made in USA: A Break in the Clouds." Address to "The Quest for Excellence" a conference sponsored by The National Institute of Standards. February 22–23, 1990. Published in *Juran Institute Papers*. CD-ROM. Juran Institute & TPOK, 1995.

"World War II and the Quality Movement." *Quality Progress* 24 (December 1991): 19–24.

"J. M. Juran: The Man Who Taught the Japanese Quality Control Talks about Caring Leadership. An Interview." *Caring People* (Spring 1992): 60–64.

"The Canoe and the Liner." Address to the University of Minnesota, Minneapolis, May 7, 1992.

"Quality in the USA: Status and Prognosis." Address at the Quality Imperative, University of Minnesota Institute of Technology, Minneapolis, May 8, 1992.

"Report on a Sentimental Journey." Address at the University of Minnesota, May 8, 1992.

"Perspectives: The Words of Dr. Juran." An interview with Judith M. Delsanter. *Total Quality Management* (May/June 1993): 5–7.

"Made in U.S.A.—A Renaissance in Quality." *Harvard Business Review* 71 (July/August 1993): 42–50.

"Juran on Quality. An Interview." *Management Review* 83 (January 1994): 11–13.

"Dr. Juran. An Interview with Tracy Benson Kirker." *Industry Week* 243 (April 4, 1994): 12–16.

"Joseph M. Juran: Our Foremost Living Quality Guru Addresses the Baldrige Award, the Business Press, the Difference between Substance and Hype, and What 'Top-Management Support' Really Means. An Interview." *Training* 31 (May 1994): 35–41.

Books

Bureaucracy: A Challenge to Better Management. New York: Harper & Brothers, 1944.

Management of Inspection and Quality Control. New York: Harper & Brothers, 1945.

Editor. *Quality Control Handbook.* 1st ed. New York: McGraw-Hill, 1951.

and Norman N. Barish. *Case Studies in Industrial Management.* New York: McGraw-Hill, 1955.

Managerial Breakthrough: A New Concept of the Manager's Job. New York: McGraw-Hill, 1964.

and J. Keith Louden. *The Corporate Director.* New York: American Management Association, 1966.

and Frank M. Gryna. *Quality Planning and Analysis: From Product Development Through Use.* 2nd ed. New York: McGraw-Hill, 1980.

and Frank M. Gryna, eds. *Juran's Quality Control Handbook.* 4th ed. New York: McGraw-Hill, 1988.

Juran on Planning for Quality. New York: Free Press, 1988.

Juran on Leadership for Quality: An Executive Handbook. New York: Free Press, 1989.

Juran on Quality by Design: The New Steps for Planning Quality into Goods and Services. New York: Free Press, 1992.

Managerial Breakthrough: The Classic Book on Improving Management Performance. 2nd ed. New York: McGraw-Hill, 1995.

Editor. *A History of Managing for Quality: The Evolution, Trends, and Future Directions of Managing for Quality.* Milwaukee: ASQC Quality Press, 1995.

Media and Unpublished Materials

Correspondence, papers, notes, and resumes. 1937–1995. Juran Institute. Wilton, Connecticut.

"Management Course: Unit No. 1, Basic Principles, Skills and Tools of Management." Seminar sponsored by the American Management Association, New York, October 6–10, 1952.

Planning and Practices in Quality Control. Lectures sponsored by Nippon Kagaku Gijutsu Renmei, Tokyo and Osaka, July/August 1954.

Juran on Quality Improvement. Juran Institute, 1980. Videotape series.

A History of Quality Control and Assurance at AT&T: 1920–1970: An Interview with Joseph M. Juran. AT&T, 1989. Videotape series.

The Last Word: Lessons of a Lifetime in Managing for Quality. Lectures sponsored by the Juran Institute, 1993.

Juran Institute Papers. CD-ROM published by TPOK and Juran Institute, 1995.

❊

OTHER SOURCES

Articles

Albright, H. F. "Fifty Years' Progress in Manufacturing." *Western Electric News* (November 1919): 22–29.

Bell Laboratories, Inspection Engineering Department. Memos and bulletins pertaining to inspection engineering and quality assurance. Location 299 09 03 06. Warren, NJ: AT&T Archives, 1927.

———. Reports from the Special Committee on Inspection Statistics and Economy, Location 250 02. Warren, NJ: AT&T Archives, 1928.

Bowles, Jerry. "W. Edwards Deming: The Man and the Legend." *The Quality Executive* (January 1994): Reprint.

Brumbaugh, Martin A., "Review of *Management of Inspection and Quality Control* by J. M. Juran." *Industrial Quality Control* 8 (July 1945): 18–19.

"Business Style Aid for Japan." *BusinessWeek,* November 14, 1953, 169–170.

Clark, Wallace. "Education of Industrial Executives in Scientific Management." In *8th International Management Congress* Vol. 1, 77–84. Stockholm: Esselte Aktiebolag, 1947.

Cohen, Jr., A. C. "Review of *Quality Control Handbook,* by J. M. Juran." *Industrial Quality Control* 8 (May 1952): 104–106.

"The Control Section: A New Aid to Management." *Modern Management* 9 (October 1949): 4–9.

"Crisis in Japan." *Time,* March 15, 1954, 94.

Day, Carl A. "Quality Control: Tool for the Manufacturing Executive." In *Joseph Juran's Japan lectures.* Original publication unknown. Date assumed to be 1952.

Dean, Arthur H. "Japan at the Crossroads." *The Atlantic Monthly* 194 (November 1954): 30–35.

Deming, W. Edwards. "What Happened in Japan?" *Industrial Quality Control* 24 (August 1967): 89–93.

"The Doctors of Management." *Fortune* 30 (July 1944): 142–146, 201–204, 207–208, 210, 213.

Dodge, H. F. "A Method of Rating Manufactured Product." *Bell System Technical Journal* 7 (April 1928): 350–368.

Drucker, Peter F. "The New Society: I. Revolution by Mass Production." *Harpers Magazine* 199 (September 1949): 21–30.

———. "Productivity Is an Attitude." *Nation's Business* 40 (April 1952): 34–36, 66–67.

———. "Politics for a New Generation. Part I: Agenda for the Next President." *Harper's Magazine* 220 (June 1960): 29–36.

———. "The Baffled Young Men of Japan." *Harper's Magazine* 222 (January 1961): 65–74.

———. "This Competitive World." *Harvard Business Review* 39 (March 1961): 131–135.

"Dueling Pioneers." *BusinessWeek,* October 25, 1991, 17.

"Executives Learn to Manage in Style." *BusinessWeek,* October 13, 1951, 98–100.

Feigenbaum, A. V. "Managing Quality Control to Encourage Quality-Mindedness." *Industrial Quality Control* 9 (May 1953): 16–20.

———. "Management of the Quality Control Function." *Industrial Quality Control* 12 (May 1956): 22–25.

————. "Total Quality Control: A New Concept of Integrated Quality Control Engineering." In *Total Quality Control in Action: Tools, Techniques and Administrative Guides* (American Management Association Management Report No. 9, 1958): 35–47.

Gabor, Andrea. "Deming Demystifies the 'Black Art' of Statistics." *Quality Progress* 24 (December 1991): 26–28.

Godfrey, A. Blanton. "The History and Evolution of Quality at AT&T." *AT&T Technical Journal* 65 (March/April 1986): 9–19.

Golomski, William A. "Walter A. Shewhart—Man of Quality—His Work, Our Challenge." *Industrial Quality Control* 24 (August 1967): 83–85.

Grant, Eugene L. and Theodore E. Lang. "Statistical Quality Control in the World War II Years." *Quality Progress* 24 (December 1991): 31–36.

Hallenbeck, Francis J. *The Inspection Engineering Department* Bell Laboratories Record 2 (August 1926): 243–247.

Haltom, Margaret Saxton. "Discrepancies in the Lend-Lease Program." *Southern Quarterly* 4 (1966): 446–468.

Henry, John A. "ASQC in Retrospect." *Quality Progress* 4 (May/June 1971): 50–53.

Hopper, Kenneth. "Creating Japan's New Industrial Management: The Americans as Teachers." *Human Resource Management* 21 (Summer 1982): 13–34.

————. "Quality, Japan, and the U.S.: The First Chapter." *Quality Progress* 18 (September 1985): 35–41.

"Japan: Approaching Desperation." *Time,* August 23, 1954, 31.

"Japan: A Tough Competitor." *BusinessWeek,* July 18, 1953, 112.

"Japan: Help Needed." *Fortune* (December 1954): 80–84.

"Japan: The Twin Blade of Crisis." *Newsweek,* November 29, 1954, 35–36.

Jones, R. L. "The Viewpoint of Inspection Engineering." *Bell Laboratories Record* 2 (August 1926): 241–242.

Kegarise, Ronald J. and George D. Miller. "An Alcoa-Kodak Joint Team." CD-ROM. TPOK/Juran Institute. 1994.

Kobayashi, Koji. "Quality Management at NEC Corporation." *Quality Progress* 19 (April 1986): 18–23.

Lorenz, M. O. "Methods of Measuring the Concentration of Wealth." *American Statistical Association* 9 (June 1905): 209–219.

Marcy, Herbert, "The Business of Making a Quality Product." *Industrial Quality Control* 5 (January 1949): 20–23.

"The M.D.'s for Management." *Newsweek,* October 28, 1957, 85–88.

"A New Start for Bausch & Lomb." *BusinessWeek,* March 7, 1953, 98–104.

Noguchi, Junji. "The Legacy of W. Edwards Deming." *Quality Progress* 28 (December 1995): 35–37.

"Now Is the Time to Economize." *Newsweek,* June 30, 1947, 56–58.

Olmstead, Paul S. "Our Debt to Walter Shewhart." *Industrial Quality Control* 24 (August 1967): 73.

Paton, Scott Madison. "Joseph M. Juran: Quality Legend." *Quality Digest* (January 1992): 32–46.

Pearson, E. S. "Some Notes on W. A. Shewhart's Influence on the Application of Statistical Methods in Great Britain." *Industrial Quality Control* 24 (August 1967): 81.

Peterson, I. A. "Review of *Management of Inspection and Quality Control,* by J. M. Juran." *Journal of the American Statistical Association* 40 (September 1945): 395–396.

"Quality Control Gets a Checkup." *BusinessWeek,* December 18, 1954, 156–157.

"The Second Annual Awarding of the Deming Prize." *Industrial Quality Control* 11 (September 1954): 3, 45.

Shewhart, W. A. "Quality Control Charts." *Bell System Technical Journal* 5 (October 1926): 593–603.

Small, Collie. "The Man with the Answers." *Nation's Business* 39 (October 1951): 51–55, 75.

Smith, Richard Austin. "Gillette Looks Sharp Again." *Fortune* 45 (June 1952): 100–103, 159–172.

Spang, Jr., J. P. "Quality Is a Business Must." *Industrial Quality Control* 5 (May 1949): 9–12.

"Statistical Quality Control." *Fortune* 40 (December 1949): 161–168.

Stratton, Brad. "Quality Goes to War: An Overview." *Quality Progress* 24 (December 1991): 18.

Stryker, Perrin. "What's Your Problem?" *Fortune* 47 (March 1953): 106–107, 183–187.

―――― . "Two Ambitious Consultants." *Fortune* 49 (May 1954): 82–85, 180–188.

"Tributes to Walter A. Shewhart." *Industrial Quality Control* 24 (August 1967): 111–122.

Tsuru, Sgigeto. "A New Japan? Political, Economic, and Social Aspects of Postwar Japan." *Atlantic Monthly* 195 (January 1955): 103–107.

Tsutsui, William M. "W. Edwards Deming and the Origins of Quality Control in Japan." *Journal of Japanese Studies* 22 (Summer 1996): 295–325.

Vertiz, Virginia C. "The Other Side of the Man of Quality: The Pearl." *Quality Progress* 28 (December 1995): 39–40.

Wallis, W. Allen. "The Statistical Research Group, 1942–1945." *Journal of the American Statistical Association* 75 (June 1980): 320–331.

Wareham, Ralph E. and Brad Stratton. "Standards, Sampling, and Schooling." *Quality Progress* 24 (December 1991): 38–42.

Western Electric. *Western Electric News.* 1905–1931.

―――― . *Microphone.* 1924–1931 and June/July1985.

―――― . "The Hawthorne Studies: A Synopsis, 1924/1974," Location 48 10 01. Warren, NJ: AT&T Archives, 1974.

"What Management Consultants Can Do." *BusinessWeek,* January 23, 1965, 88–104.

Working, Holbrook. "Statistical Quality Control in War Production." *Journal of the American Statistical Association* 40 (December 1945): 425–447.

Books

Adams, Russell. *The Man and His Wonderful Shaving Device: King Gillette.* Boston: Little, Brown and Company, 1978.

Adams, Stephen. Unpublished, work-in-progress manuscript about the history of Western Electric. 1996.

Aguayo, Rafael. *Dr. Deming: The Man Who Taught the Japanese About Quality.* New York: Lyle Smart, 1990.

Barnes, Ralph M., and James S. Perkins with the assistance of Joseph M. Juran. *A Study of the Effect of Practice on the Elements of a Factory Operation.* Studies in Engineering, Bulletin 22. Iowa City: University of Iowa, 1940.

Beasley, W. G. *The Rise of Modern Japan.* 2nd ed. New York: St. Martin's Press, 1995.

Capezio, Peter, and Debra Morehouse. *Taking the Mystery Out of TQM: A Practical Guide to Total Quality Management.* 2nd ed. Franklin Lakes, New Jersey: Career Press, 1995.

Chandler, Jr., Alfred. *The Visible Hand: The Managerial Revolution in American Business.* Cambridge: Belknap Press of Harvard University, 1977.

Chandler, Jr., Alfred, and Herman Daems, eds. *Managerial Hierarchies: Comparative Perspectives on the Rise of the Modern Industrial Enterprise.* Cambridge: Harvard University Press, 1980.

Clark, Wallace. *The Gantt Chart.* New York: The Ronald Press Company, 1922.

Cohen, Theodore. *Remaking Japan: The American Occupation as New Deal.* New York: The Free Press, 1987.

Collins, James C., and Jerry I. Porras. *Built to Last: Successful Habits of Visionary Companies.* New York: HarperBusiness, 1994.

Council on Foreign Relations. *The Problem of Lend-Lease: Its Nature, Implications, and Settlement.* New York: Council on Foreign Relations, 1944.

Crosby, Philip B. *Quality Is Free: The Art of Making Quality Certain.* New York: Mentor, 1980.

————. *Quality Is Still Free: Making Quality Certain in Uncertain Times.* New York: McGraw-Hill, 1996.

Deming, W. Edwards. *The Elementary Principles of the Statistical Control of Quality, A Series of Lectures.* Tokyo: Nippon Kagaku Gijutsu Remmei, 1951.

———. *Out of the Crisis.* Cambridge: M.I.T. Center for Advanced Engineering Study, 1982.

Dobyns, Lloyd, and Clare Crawford-Mason. *Thinking About Quality: Progress, Wisdom, and the Deming Philosophy.* New York: Times Books, 1994.

Dougherty, James J. *The Politics of Wartime Aid.* Westport, CT: Greenwood Press, 1978.

Drucker, Peter F. *The Practice of Management: A Study of the Most Important Function in American Society.* New York: Harper & Row, 1954.

———. *Adventures of a Bystander.* New York: Harper & Row, 1979.

Duncan, W. Jack. *Great Ideas in Management: Lessons from the Founders and Foundations of Managerial Practice.* San Francisco: Jossey-Bass, 1989.

Duus, Peter. *The Rise of Modern Japan.* Boston: Houghton Mifflin Co., 1976.

Fagen, M. D., editor, *A History of Engineering and Science in the Bell System: The Early Years (1875–1925).* New York: Bell Telephone Laboratories, 1975.

Gabor, Andrea. *The Man Who Discovered Quality: How W. Edwards Deming Brought the Quality Revolution to America—The Stories of Ford, Xerox, and GM.* New York: Penguin Books, 1992.

Gantt, Henry. *Gantt on Management: Guidelines for Today's Executive.* Edited by Alex W. Rathe. New York: American Management Association, The American Society of Engineers, 1961.

Garvin, David. *Managing Quality: The Strategic and Competitive Edge.* New York: Free Press, 1988.

General Headquarters Supreme Commander for the Allied Powers and Far East Command. *Selected Data on the Occupation of Japan.* 1950.

Gibney, Frank. *Miracle by Design: The Real Reasons Behind Japan's Economic Success.* New York: Times Books, 1982.

Gillespie, Richard. *Manufacturing Knowledge: A History of the Hawthorne Experiments.* Cambridge: Cambridge University Press, 1991.

Goodwin, Doris Kearns. *No Ordinary Time: Franklin and Eleanor Roosevelt: The Home Front in World War II.* New York: Simon & Schuster, 1994.

Goonan, Kathleen Jennison. *The Juran Prescription: Clinical Quality Management.* San Francisco: Jossey-Bass, 1995.

Gordon, Albert. *Jews in Transition.* Minneapolis: University of Minnesota Press, 1949.

Halberstam, David. *The Reckoning.* New York: William Morrow and Co., 1986.

Hamel, Gary, and C. K. Prahalad. *Competing for the Future.* Boston: Harvard Business School Press, 1994.

Herring, George C. "An Experiment in Foreign Aid: Lend-Lease, 1941–1945." Ph.D. Dissertation, University of Virginia, 1965.

Hounshell, David A. *From the American System to Mass Production, 1800–1932: The Development of Manufacturing Technology in the United States.* Baltimore: Johns Hopkins University Press, 1984.

Huczynski, Andrzej A. *Management Gurus: What Makes Them and How to Become One.* London: Routledge, 1993.

Ishikawa, Kaoru. *What Is Total Quality Control? The Japanese Way.* Translated by David J. Lu. Englewood Cliffs, NJ: Prentice Hall, Inc., 1985.

Juran, Nathan, *Foot Loose in the World.* Self published. 1992.

Kamiya, Shotaro. *My Life with Toyota.* Translated by Thomas I. Elliott. Japan: Toyota Motor Sales Company, 1976.

Kanter, Rosabeth Moss. *The Change Masters: Innovation and Entrepreneurship in the American Corporation.* New York: Simon & Schuster, 1984.

Killian, Cecelia S. *The World of W. Edwards Deming.* 2nd ed. Knoxville: SPC Press, 1992.

Kimball, Warren. *The Most Unsordid Act: Lend Lease, 1939–1941.* Johns Hopkins Press, 1969.

Manchester, William. *American Caesar: Douglas MacArthur 1880–1964.* Boston: Little, Brown and Co., 1978.

Mayo, Elton. *The Human Problems of an Industrial Civilization.* New York: The Macmillan Company, 1933. Reprint. Salem, New Hampshire: Ayer Company, 1992.

Mead, Margaret, ed. *Cultural Patterns and Technical Change*. Deventer, Holland: UNESCO, 1953.

Micklethwait, John, and Adrian Wooldridge. *The Witch Doctors: Making Sense of the Management Gurus*. New York: Times Books, 1996.

Millman, S., editor, *A History of Engineering Science in the Bell System: Communications Science (1925–1980)*. New York: AT&T Bell Laboratories, 1984.

Nelson, Daniel, *Managers and Workers: Origins of the New Factory System in the United States, 1880–1920*. Madison: The University of Wisconsin Press, 1975.

Noble, David F. *America By Design: Science, Technology, and the Rise of Corporate Capitalism*. New York: Alfred A. Knopf, 1977.

Page, Arthur W. *The Bell Telephone System*. New York: Harper Brothers, 1941.

Peters, Thomas J., and Robert H. Waterman, Jr. *In Search of Excellence: Lessons from America's Best-Run Companies*. New York: Warner Books, 1982.

Pook, Ronald. *Tales of Hawthorne: 1919–1947,* Location 44 11 01. Warren, NJ: AT&T Archives, 1988. Unpublished manuscript.

President of the United States. *Twentieth Report to Congress on Lend-Lease Operations, for the Period Ended June 30, 1945,* 1945.

Reich, Leonard S. *The Making of American Industrial Research: Science and Business at GE and Bell, 1876–1926*. Cambridge: Cambridge University Press, 1985.

Roethlisberger. F. J., and William Dickson. *Management and the Worker*. Cambridge, Harvard University Press, 1939.

Sarasohn, Homer M., and Charles W. Protzman. *CCS: Industrial Management* (photocopy). Baker Library, Harvard University, 1949.

Seder, Leonard A. "Quality Control in Screw Machine Operations" In *Quality Control Handbook*. Edited by Joseph M. Juran. 1st ed. New York: McGraw-Hill, 1951.

Shewhart, Walter A. *Economic Control of Quality of Manufactured Product*. New York: D. Van Nostrand, 1931. Reprint. Milwaukee: ASQC Quality Press, 1980.

———— . *Statistical Method from the Viewpoint of Quality Control.* Edited by W. Edwards Deming. Washington, DC: Graduate School of the Department of Agriculture, 1939. Reprint with new foreword by W. Edwards Deming. New York: Dover Publications, 1986.

Sloan, Jr., Alfred P. *My Years with General Motors.* Edited by John McDonald with Catharine Stevens. New York: Anchor Book Press, 1972.

Smith, George David. *The Anatomy of a Business Strategy: Bell, Western Electric and the Origins of the American Telephone Industry.* Baltimore: Johns Hopkins University, 1985.

Stettinius, Edward R. "Report to the President, On Operations of the Lend-Lease Administration, September 11, 1941 to September 25, 1943." (Government document).

———— . *Lend-Lease, Weapon for Victory.* New York: Macmillan Co., 1944.

Taylor, Frederick Winslow. *The Principles of Scientific Management.* 1911. Reprint. New York: W.W. Norton, 1967.

von Auw, Alvin. *Heritage & Destiny: Reflections on the Bell System in Transition.* New York, Praeger, 1983.

Walton, Mary. *The Deming Management Method.* New York: Perigee Books, 1986.

Whitsett, David A., and Lyle Yorks. *From Management Theory to Business Sense: The Myths and Realities of People at Work.* New York: AMACOM, 1983.

Womack, James P., and Daniel T. Jones. *Lean Thinking: Banish Waste and Create Wealth in Your Corporation.* New York: Simon & Schuster, 1996.

Womack, James P., Daniel T. Jones, and Daniel Roos. *The Machine That Changed the World.* New York: Harper Perennial, 1990.

Wrege, Charles D., and Ronald G. Greenwood. *Frederick W. Taylor: The Father of Scientific Management, Myth and Reality.* Homewood, IL: Business One Irwin, 1991.

Wren, Daniel. *The Evolution of Management Thought.* 3rd ed. New York: John Wiley & Sons, 1987.

Zuboff, Shoshana. *In the Age of the Smart Machine: The Future of Work and Power.* New York: Basic Books, 1988.

Interviews

Appley, Lawrence. Interview by Howland Blackiston and Jack Schatz, October 24, 1991. Hamilton, New York.

Blackiston, Howland. Interview by John Butman, June 11, 1996. Wilton, Connecticut.

Blackiston, Joy, Granddaughter. Interview by Howland Blackiston and Jack Schatz, May 2, 1991. Wilton, Connecticut.

Crosby, Philip A. Telephone interview by John Butman, October 14, 1996.

Deming, W. Edwards. Interview by Howland Blackiston and Jack Schatz, April 10, 1991. Washington, DC.

Drucker, Peter. Interview by Howland Blackiston and Jack Schatz, December 20, 1991. Claremont, California.

Feigenbaum, Armand V. Telephone interview by John Butman, December 27, 1996.

Galvin, Robert. Interview by Howland Blackiston and Jack Schatz, June 19, 1992. Chicago, Illinois.

Germain, Jack. Interview by Howland Blackiston and Jack Schatz, June 19, 1992. Chicago, Illinois.

Godfrey, A. Blanton. Interview by Howland Blackiston and Jack Schatz, May 2, 1991. Wilton, Connecticut.

————— . Interview by John Butman, June 11, 1996. Wilton, Connecticut.

Goldberg, Minerva Juran. Interview by Howland Blackiston and Jack Schatz, October 25, 1991. Williamsville, New York.

Gryna, Jr., Frank M. Interview by Howland Blackiston and Jack Schatz, May 2, 1991. Wilton, Connecticut.

————— . Telephone interview by John Butman, December 1996.

Hartman, Gerald. Interview by Howland Blackiston and Jack Schatz, October 29, 1991. Atlanta, Georgia.

Hawthornthwaite, Brian. Interview by Howland Blackiston and Jack Schatz, October 29, 1991. Atlanta, Georgia.

Hutchins, David. Interview by Howland Blackiston and Jack Schatz, April 7, 1992. Amsterdam, The Netherlands.

Imaizumi, M. Interview by Howland Blackiston and Jack Schatz, March 16, 1992. Tokyo, Japan.

Jobs, Stephen P. Interview by Howland Blackiston and Jack Schatz, December 19, 1991. Redwood City, California.

Juran, Charles E., Son. Interview by Howland Blackiston and Jack Schatz, May 24, 1991. Palos Verdes, California.

Juran, Donald, Son. Interview by Howland Blackiston and Jack Schatz, May 2, 1991. Wilton, Connecticut.

Juran, Joseph M. Interview by John Larson, 1974. Minneapolis, Minnesota.

————. Interview by Howland Blackiston and Jack Schatz, March 6, 1991. Wilton, Connecticut.

————. Interview by Howland Blackiston and Jack Schatz, May 2, 1991. Wilton, Connecticut.

————. Interview by Howland Blackiston and Jack Schatz, June 14, 1991. Ridgefield, Connecticut.

————. Interview by Howland Blackiston and Jack Schatz, June 16, 1993. Minneapolis, Minnesota.

————. Interview by John Butman, June 19, 1996. Ridgefield, Connecticut.

————. Interview by John Butman and John De Lancey, October 29, 1996. Ridgefield, Connecticut.

Juran, Mrs. J. M., Wife. Interview by Howland Blackiston and Jack Schatz, June 14, 1991. Ridgefield, Connecticut.

Juran, Nathan H., Brother. Interview by Howland Blackiston and Jack Schatz, May 24, 1991. Palos Verdes Estates, California.

————. Interview by John De Lancey, July 14, 1996. Palos Verdes Estates, California.

Juran, Sylvia, Daughter. Interview by Howland Blackiston and Jack Schatz, May 2, 1991. Wilton, Connecticut.

Kano, Noriaki. Interview by Howland Blackiston and Jack Schatz, August 28, 1991. Wilton, Connecticut.

Karatsu, Hajime. Interview by Howland Blackiston and Jack Schatz, March 18, 1992. Tokyo, Japan.

Kegarise, Ron. Interview by Howland Blackiston and Jack Schatz, October 29, 1991. Atlanta, Georgia.

Kondo, Yoshio. Interview by Howland Blackiston and Jack Schatz, March 18, 1992. Tokyo, Japan.

Kume, Hitoshi. Interview by Howland Blackiston and Jack Schatz, March 17, 1992. Tokyo, Japan.

Luther, David. Interview by Howland Blackiston and Jack Schatz, April 7, 1992. Amsterdam, The Netherlands.

Mayor, Peg Juran, Granddaughter. Interview by Howland Blackiston and Jack Schatz, June 14, 1991. Ridgefield, Connecticut.

Mihauchi, Ichiro. Interview by Howland Blackiston and Jack Schatz, March 16, 1992. Tokyo, Japan.

Nakada, Yoshinao. Interview by Howland Blackiston and Jack Schatz, March 19, 1992. Tokyo, Japan.

Noguchi, Jungi. Interview by Howland Blackiston and Jack Schatz, March 16, 1992. Tokyo, Japan.

Onnais, Arturo. Interview by Howland Blackiston and Jack Schatz, April 7, 1992. Amsterdam, The Netherlands.

Petree, Richard. Telephone interview by John Butman, January 7, 1997.

Sandholm, Lennart. Interview by Howland Blackiston and Jack Schatz, October 29, 1991. Atlanta, Georgia.

Sarasohn, Homer M. Telephone interview by John Butman, December 9, 1996.

Scanlon, Robert. Interview by Howland Blackiston and Jack Schatz, October 29, 1991. Atlanta, Georgia.

Scott, Brian. Interview by Howland Blackiston and Jack Schatz, May 10, 1992. New York, New York.

Seder, Leonard. Interview by John De Lancey, November 13, 1996. Lexington, Massachusetts.

Shainin, Dorian. Telephone interview by John Butman, January 10, 1997.

Shnitzler, Meyer. Interview by John De Lancey, November 13, 1996. Lexington, Massachusetts.

Sterret, Kent. Interview by Howland Blackiston and Jack Schatz, October 29, 1991. Atlanta, Georgia.

Stoner, James F. July 18, 1992. New York, New York.

Stratton, Brad. Interview by Howland Blackiston and Jack Schatz, October 29, 1991. Atlanta, Georgia.

Sutherland, Laura. Interview by Howland Blackiston and Jack Schatz, August 28, 1991. Wilton, Connecticut.

Taguchi, Genichi. Interview by Howland Blackiston and Jack Schatz, March 19, 1992. Tokyo, Japan.

Takeshi Ken Kayano. Interview by Howland Blackiston and Jack Schatz, March 16, 1992. Tokyo, Japan.

Tilley, Brian. Interview by Howland Blackiston and Jack Schatz, August 28, 1991. Wilton, Connecticut.

Vernais, Matthis. Interview by Howland Blackiston and Jack Schatz, April 7, 1992. Amsterdam, The Netherlands.

Watanabe, Eizo. Interview by Howland Blackiston and Jack Schatz, March 16, 1992. Tokyo, Japan.

Zeynel, Charles. Interview by Howland Blackiston and Jack Schatz, October 29, 1991. Atlanta, Georgia.

Media

An Immigrant's Gift: The Life of Quality Pioneer Joseph M. Juran. Weston, CT: WoodsEnd, 1996. Videotape.

ASQC. "Joseph M. Juran: A Search for Universal Principles." ASQC Home Page. July 1, 1995.

AT&T. *A History of Quality Control and Assurance at AT&T: 1920–1970: An Interview with W. Edwards Deming,* 1989. Videotape.

If Japan Can . . . Why Can't We? NBC, 1980. Videotape.

Frey, Larry. *Joseph M. Juran: Growing Up in Minneapolis.* August, 1994. Slide Show narrative for a testimonial dinner for Dr. Juran by the Minnesota Section, ASQC, June 15, 1993.

Index